# THINK HISTORY! 1

## CHANGING TIMES
## 1066–1500

Martin Collier   Steve Day   Barry Doherty   Bill Marriott

Series editor: Lindsay von Elbing

**heinemann.co.uk**
✓ Free online support
✓ Useful weblinks
✓ 24 hour online ordering

**01865 888080**

Heinemann Educational Publishers
Halley Court, Jordan Hill, Oxford, OX2 8EJ
Part of Harcourt Education

Heinemann is the registered trademark of
Harcourt Education Limited

© Martin Collier, Steve Day, Barry Doherty, Bill Marriott, 2003.

First published 2003
07 06
10 9 8 7 6 5

British Library Cataloguing in Publication Data is available from the British Library on request.

10-digit ISBN: 0 435 31334 7
13-digit ISBN: 978 0 435313 34 7

Produced by IFA Design Ltd
Printed in Spain by Mateu Cromo s.a.
Picture research by Frances Topp
Illustrations on page 116 by Paul Bale

**Photographic acknowledgements**
The authors and publisher would like to thank the following for permission to reproduce photographs:
Aerofilms: 66A; AKG: 44C, 183C, 196C; Alamy: 79B; Ancient Art and Architecture: 20D, 29 (top), 103B, 104C; Ancient
Art and Architecture/L. Ellison: 8C; Art Archive: 78A, 142B; Art Archive/British Library: 157E; Bibliothèque Nationale
de France: 148E, 191F, 192G; Bridgeman: 79C, 85F, 107C, 174 (bottom) 196B; Bridgeman/House of Commons: 149F;
British Library: 113A, 137A, 137B, 141A, 148D; British Library/Bridgeman: 57A (Cott. Faust B VII f.72v); British
Museum: 146A; Cambridge University: 193I; Corbis: 10B, 17A; Corpus Christi College, Cambridge: 154C;
Courtauld/Conway Library/Corpus Christi College, Cambridge: 148C; Dean & Chapter of Durham Cathedral: 57B;
English Heritage: 48–9, 69A; Fortean Picture Library: 129A; Fotomas: 90B; Getty News: 153A; Hampshire Court
Records: 185F; Hulton: 156D, 178C, 191E, 192H; Lambeth Palace Library, London: 117C; Mansell Collection: 50A;
Mary Evans Picture Library: 38A; Michael Holford: 66C, 103A; NASA: 10A; PA News: 153B; Penshurst Palace: 164B;
Peter Evans: 163A; Photofusion: 93B, 93C; Rex: 24A; Robert Estall Photos: 66B; Robert Harding: 180F; Scala: 190C;
Sheridan/Ancient Art and Architecture: 83E; Sonia Halliday: 104D, 123B, 127F, 166E; Trinity College Cambridge: 98A;
Trip: 93A
Source unknown: 19B, 20C, 22E, 29 (bottom), 30, 40, 89A, 107A, 107B, 108D, 117B, 147B, 174A, 177A

Cover photograph: © British Library. The picture is 'An army being transported in ships', c. fifteenth century.

**Written source acknowledgements**
The author and publisher gratefully acknowledge the following publications from which written sources in the
book are drawn. In some sentences the wording or sentence structure has been simplified:
R. Allen Brown, *The Normans and the Norman Conquest* (Constable, 1968): 61D;
I. Coulson and I. Dawson, *Medicine and Health Through Time* (John Murray, 1996): 82D;
C. Culpin and I. Dawson, *The Norman Conquest* (John Murray, 2002): 70B;
J. Nichol, *Thinking History: Medieval Realms* (Blackwell, 1991): 82C;
S. Sancha, *Lincoln Castle: The Medieval Story* (Lincolnshire County Council, 1985): 71D;
ed. Lesley Smith, *The Making of Britain: The Middle Ages* (Macmillan, 1985): 165D, 167G;
A. Williams, *The English and the Norman Conquest* (Boydell, 1995): 60C

Tel: 01865 888058  www.heinemann.co.uk

# CONTENTS

# DID HAROLD DESERVE TO LOSE THE ENGLISH THRONE?

*You are about to begin a journey of discovery. By the end of this chapter, you will know and understand a lot more about the crisis that affected England nearly 1000 years ago. You will also be able to answer some key questions about this time.*

💡 *Why have people always wanted to invade Britain?*

💡 *Why did the death of a king push England into a period of war and chaos?*

## TIMELINE
## 6500 BC to AD 1066

| | |
|---|---|
| **6500 BC** | The first humans settle in the British Isles. |
| **500 BC** | The Celts begin to arrive from northern Europe. |
| **AD 42** | The Romans begin their invasion of Britain. |
| **AD 360** | Barbarian armies begin to invade Roman Britain. |
| **AD 410** | Roman Britain ends as Angles, Saxons and other invaders attack England and Wales. |
| **AD 750** | The Vikings begin raids and set up control over most of northern and eastern England. |
| **AD 937** | Anglo-Saxon rule is restored under King Athelstan. |
| **AD 980** | The Danish Vikings launch attacks on England. |
| **AD 1016** | The first of three Viking kings begin to rule England. |
| **AD 1042** | King Edward the Confessor is crowned the first English king in 26 years. |
| **AD 1066** | Harold Godwin is defeated at the Battle of Hastings by Duke William of Normandy. |

# WHO INVADED BRITAIN BEFORE 1066 AND WHY?

By the end of this section you will be able to answer these questions.
- Why was Britain attractive to early invaders?
- Who invaded Britain between 500 BC and AD 1016?
- How was Britain changed by these invaders?
- How settled were the people of Britain before 1066?
You will find evidence to back up your ideas about the invaders.

## Starter

*With a partner, make a list of any nations you think have ever invaded Britain.*

## Britain: a land worthy of invasion

Britain has not been invaded now for nearly 950 years. Many people do not realise that Britain was once attractive to many invaders. The first humans arrived in what we today call Britain about 8500 years ago. These Stone Age people were probably drawn here by the thick forests, wild animals and stories about being able to find precious metals like gold, silver and tin in the rocks. The first major settlers who came in large numbers were the Celts. They began to arrive about 500 BC. The Celts were well known for their unusual religious practices, their worship of nature and their frightening appearance in battle.

SOURCE (A)

Most of the tribes living inland do not grow grain. They live on milk and meat, and wear skins. All the Britons dye their bodies with **woad**, which makes them look wild – especially in battle. They wear their hair long. But every other part of their body, except the upper lip, they shave.

**A description of the Celts in 55 BC by the Roman emperor, Julius Caesar.**

### Key words

**Woad** A plant that gives a blue dye.

The Roman Empire was expanding throughout Europe, which brought the threat of attack closer towards Britain. In AD 42, the Romans launched a full-scale attack. By AD 84 they had completely conquered the whole of England and Wales up to Hadrian's Wall, along the border with Scotland.

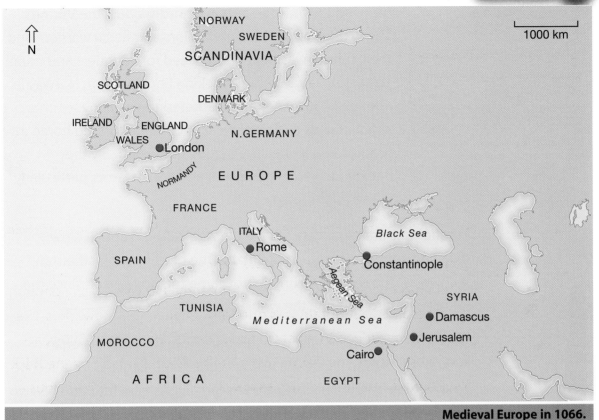

**Medieval Europe in 1066.**

With the Romans came a long period of prosperity to southern Britain. Beautiful public buildings, modern villas, libraries and roads changed the lives of those who lived in Britain. The Romans also brought Christianity to Britain. This had a dramatic impact on English laws, culture, architecture and literature. However, by the beginning of the fifth century AD, the power of the Roman Empire was fading and Britain once again became a target for attack.

## The new invaders

### The Anglo-Saxons

From AD 360, new invaders began to raid and then settle along the British coastline, slowly moving inland and controlling the whole country. Many came from Denmark and northern Germany. They were known as the Anglo-Saxons. These invaders eventually married into Roman and Celtic families, and a kind of peace was restored.

## Key words

**Scandinavia** An area of land that includes Denmark, Norway and Sweden.

**Viking** Invaders from Scandinavia.

**Monasteries** Large buildings that were home to Christian monks. Monasteries were often filled with gold, silver and precious stones.

### The Vikings

But there were even more invaders. A new power was growing towards the east in **Scandinavia** – the **Vikings**. The Vikings were very good sailors and fierce warriors, and their culture was built on the need for conquest and trade. The first Vikings began attacking England from Norway in about AD 750. At first they targeted the wealthy **monasteries** and royal palaces before returning home to Scandinavia as wealthy heroes. But eventually they decided to settle in England and set up farms, particularly in the north and east.

Throughout the tenth century, the old Anglo-Saxon armies slowly regained control over much of Britain. One of its leaders, Athelstan (known as 'The King of All Britain'), became the first person since the Roman emperors to rule the whole country.

From AD 980 yet more Vikings – this time from Denmark – began raiding the English coast. The Vikings conquered England for a second time. Between 1016 and 1042 three Viking kings – Canute, and his two sons Harefoot and Harthacanute – ruled England.

In 1042 England was ruled by another Englishman, Edward the Confessor. But would he be the last English king? Or would England be attacked by yet another foreign army?

### SOURCE C

Viking long ships, like this one, allowed the Vikings to travel as far as Greenland and North America.

# TASKS...

1 Rearrange the settlers below to show the order in which they arrived in Britain between 6500 BC and AD 980. Write down your answer in your book.

**Vikings**        **Romans**        **Stone Age**        **Anglo-Saxons**        **Celts**

2 **a)** What problems might the settlers have caused the people of Britain?

   **b)** What benefits might the settlers have brought to the people of Britain?

3 What questions would you ask to find out more about the people who lived in Britain many hundreds of years ago? In pairs, make a list. Compare your list with other pairs in your class.

## Plenary

Work in pairs to complete the definitions table. The first person can pick any of the definitions. The second person should give the correct term for that definition. Now swap jobs!

| DEFINITIONS | TERMS |
|---|---|
| Precious metals found in Britain. | Celts |
| It covered most of Britain one thousand years ago. | Christianity |
| A time when no one used metal. | monasteries |
| The first major group of settlers. | gold and silver |
| Built to keep the Scots out of England. | Hadrian's Wall |
| A large Roman house. | Harthacnut |
| A new religion brought by the Romans. | Anglo-Saxons |
| They came from Denmark and Germany. | Athelstan |
| They enjoyed fighting and trading. | forest |
| Target of the Vikings. | Vikings |
| The 'King of All Britain'. | Stone Age |
| The last Viking king in Britain. | villa |

You could also try choosing a term and working out the definition that goes with it.

# WHAT WERE THE KEY EVENTS IN THE LIFE OF KING EDWARD?

By the end of this section you will be able to answer these questions.
- Who was Edward the Confessor?
- How did he become king against all the odds?
- Did it matter that he had no children?
- Who became king when he died?
- Why was the new king such a problem?

You will evaluate events in Edward's life and create a living graph.

## SOURCE A

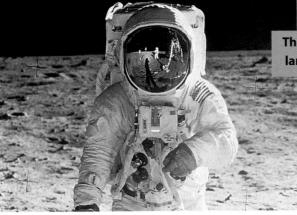

The first moon landing, 1969.

## Starter

*Look at Sources A and B which are both well-known moments in history.*

## SOURCE B

The terrorist attack on the World Trade Centre in New York, 11 September 2001.

- *Do you think the events shown in Sources A and B are important moments in our history?*

- *How do you think people reacted to the news of these two events?*

- *How do you think the world changed after these events?*

- *Which of these events do you think will be forgotten first?*

- *Do you think the world can change forever after a single event?*

# How was Edward's life turned ndsɪpə pomu?

One year stands out from all other years in the history of the British Isles: 1066. This was when the Battle of Hastings and the Norman Conquest of England happened. Historians have called this year a 'watershed', a 'turning point' and a 'landmark' in history.

What do you think these three words mean?

Read the story of Edward's life. There are questions at the end of each section. **WS**

### Edward's early years

Edward was born into a rich and powerful royal family. His father was Ethelred, King of England. His mother, Emma, was the sister of Duke Richard of Normandy. As a young boy, Edward enjoyed the life of a wealthy prince. He often played and hunted with his older brother, Alfred, and his younger sister, Goda. However, Edward's happiness was about to end…

In 1013 and again in 1016, the **Danes** successfully attacked England. The stress was too much for King Ethelred, who died suddenly in 1016. Emma, his widow, wisely took her two sons and daughter to Normandy to seek refuge with her brother Richard, the Duke. Edward spoke little Norman French at this time. So he must have felt like a stranger and a nuisance in the cold and draughty Norman castle.

> ### Key words
>
> **Danes** Viking invaders from Denmark.

Why do you think Edward might have felt frightened as he sat in the Norman castle?

### Edward's return to England

After Ethelred's death, England was ruled by a new king. He was a tough and fearless Viking from Denmark called Canute.

Following orders from her brother, Emma returned to England and was forced to marry Canute, her dead husband's old rival! Almost immediately the couple had a son, Harthacanute.

In 1035, King Canute died. His two sons began fighting about who would take over the English throne. The eldest son was Harefoot, from Canute's first marriage to a Danish princess called Elgiva. The second son was Harthacanute, from his second marriage to Emma. Harthacanute was the clear favourite with powerful people like Queen Emma, the **Archbishop of Canterbury** and the Godwin family of Wessex. This dispute almost pushed England into a bloody **civil war**.

In the middle of all this unrest and arguing, Queen Emma encouraged her other two sons, Alfred and Edward, to return to England and reclaim the throne for themselves. Edward got as far as Southampton, but quickly retreated when he found that he wasn't welcome. Alfred was not so lucky. He was discovered and captured by **Earl** Godwin's men, and was then murdered with a red-hot poker. Throughout the rest of Edward's life, he always blamed Earl Godwin for his brother's death.

Harefoot ruled for five years, from 1035 to 1040. When he died, his half-brother, Harthacanute, ruled for two more years. They were the last Viking kings of England.

💡 Why do you think Edward and Alfred wanted to return to England?

### Edward marries

In 1042, Edward saw a chance to be King of England – just like his father. However, he had rivals for the throne. First, there was King Magnus of Norway. Second, there was King Svein Estrithson of Denmark. But both were too busy fighting one another to sail to England and claim the throne.

When Edward arrived in England from Normandy he married Edith Godwin, the daughter of the most powerful earl in England, and claimed the English throne.

## Family tree

**Richard I, Duke of Normandy**

- Richard II, = Estrith
Duke of Normandy
- Elgiva [1] = **Canute I, King of England (1016–35)** = [2] Emma [1] = **Ethelred II, King of England (979–1016)**
- Godwin, Earl of Wessex (d.1053)

- Robert, Duke of Normandy
- **Harold Harefoot, King of England (1035–40)**  **Harthacanute, King of England (1040–2)**
- Alfred   Goda
- **Edward the Confessor, King of England (1042–66)** = Edith Godwin   **Harold I, King of England (1066)**   Tostig

- **William I, the Conqueror (1066–87)**

**Family tree showing the links between the Norman and English families.**

💡 Why do you think Edward married the daughter of his old enemy?

💡 Do you think it was luck or clever judgement that Edward became king? Explain your answer.

### Edward and religion

In 1051, Edward fell out with the Godwin family. He had always blamed them for his brother's death. For a year, the whole Godwin family hid in Europe, but they returned a year later to receive a full pardon from King Edward. During this time, Edith was stripped of all her royal titles and privileges, and thrown into a **convent**. King Edward was a very religious man. In fact, he was so religious that he became known as 'Edward the Confessor.'

### Key words

**Convent** A place where nuns are trained and live.

💡 Can you work out why he was known as Edward the Confessor?

When Earl Godwin died the following year, Edward granted him a full state funeral – like that of a king. Many people thought that the Godwins were, in fact, the new royal family and would soon become future kings of England – especially Harold, Earl Godwin's son.

The old hatred Edward felt towards the Godwins seemed to disappear by the early 1060s. Harold Godwin (Earl of Wessex and brother of Edith) proved to be very loyal. Edward became so reliant on Harold that he named him '**subregulus**'. This was a huge honour.

Edward and Edith did not have any children during their 20-year marriage. But throughout Edward's reign he named many people as his **heir**. These included King Svein Estrithson of Denmark, Prince Edward the Atheling (Edward's great nephew), Duke William of Normandy and Harold Godwin. It was a great honour to be named as Edward's heir. However, these promises didn't mean much because only the **Witan** could name a new king of England.

- Do you think Edward forgave the Godwins for his brother's death? Explain your answer.

- Why do you think the Godwins might have been regarded as England's royal family?

- Why do you think Edward promised the throne to so many people?

### Edward dies

On Christmas Eve 1065, Edward had a stroke. As heavy snow settled all around the king's castle, Harold and Edith, the Witan and leading churchmen gathered around Edward's bed to hear his final words. Awaking from a long sleep, Edward warned of future trouble for England. Then, looking at Harold and pointing at Edith, he said:

*'I commend this woman and all the kingdom to your protection'.*

> ## Key words
>
> **Subregulus** Deputy king.
>
> **Heir** The person who will be the next king or queen.
>
> **Witan** A council of noblemen that advised English kings.
>
> **Coronation** When a person is crowned king or queen.

Harold had been named by Edward as his successor, a choice that was immediately backed by the whole Witan. Edward lived long enough to see Westminster Abbey, his lifelong work, completed, but he died on 5 January 1066.

On 6 January 1066, Edward was buried in Westminster Abbey and Harold was crowned King of England. Harold's pride and happiness must have been partly spoiled by the knowledge that many foreign kings, dukes and princes were unhappy about his **coronation**.

# TASKS...

**1** Think about who's who in the story of Edward. In your book, write a sentence to explain what you now know about these characters.

| | | |
|---|---|---|
| **Edward** | **King Canute** | **Earl Godwin** |
| **Harefoot** | **Harthacanute** | **William**           **Edward the Atheling** |

**2** Below are the key moments in the life of Edward the Confessor. The story you have just read will help you to arrange these events into chronological (time) order.

   **a)** News reaches Edward of his brother's capture and horrific death.

   **b)** Edward and his army are forced to retreat from Southampton.

   **c)** Edward's mother marries King Canute, his father's old enemy. They have a son called Harthacanute.

   **d)** On his deathbed, Edward names Harold Godwin as his successor.

   **e)** Edward finally becomes king in 1042.

   **f)** Edward and Edith fail to produce any children.

   **g)** Edward's father dies and the family is forced to flee to Normandy.

   **h)** Edward marries Edith, brother of Harold Godwin, in 1045.

   **i)** The young Edward lives in London with his brother, sister, mother and father – who is King of England.

   **j)** Edward grows up among strangers in a Norman castle.

**3** Use statements (a) to (j) in Task 1 to produce a living graph for Edward. Try to decide which moments were the happiest in his life and which were the saddest. **WS**

Happiest moments ↑

Saddest moments ↓

Birth                                                    Death

Try to explain why you have put these moments where you have.

* What do you think were the two happiest moments in Edward's life?
* What do you think were the two saddest moments?
  Discuss your ideas in pairs, then with other class members.

**4** Find examples in the story of Edward's life that suggest he was indecisive, cruel, lonely, frightened and lucky. Put these headings in your book and summarise under each an example from the story of Edward's life.

## Plenary

Discuss the following questions.

### Knowledge

a)  Who do you think were Edward's close relatives?

b)  Which people did Edward rely on throughout his life?

### Understanding

c)  Why do you think Edward married Edith Godwin?

d)  Why do you think Edward promised the throne to so many people?

### Speculation and guesswork

e)  Do you think Emma deserved to be stripped of all her royal titles and privileges and thrown into a convent?

f)  Do you think any rulers of foreign countries would dare to challenge Harold's claim to the throne?

# KEY CONTENDERS: WHO HAD THE GREATEST CLAIM TO THE ENGLISH THRONE?

Objectives

By the end of this section you will have looked at evidence to find out:

- How many **contenders** were there to the English throne?
- Why did each contender think that they should be king?

You will be able to carry out a SWOT analysis. This will enable you to analyse:

- Whose claim to the throne was the greatest?
- To what extent each contender was able to try and win the crown?

## Starter

*In 1912, the* Titanic *sank to the bottom of the ocean. On board were priceless pieces of jewellery, works of art and other* **artefacts**, *precious metals and personal belongings worth millions of pounds – not to mention the bodies of more than 1500 people who drowned.*

### Key words

**Contender** Someone who is in competition with others for something.

**Artefact** Something man-made that has become precious.

SOURCE A

The *Titanic* sank in the Atlantic Ocean in 1912.

17

*In pairs, look at Source A. Now imagine that a very rich person has built a ship capable of pulling the* Titanic *from the sea bed.*

💡 *Think about how much all the things that sunk with the ship might be worth.*

💡 *List all the people who you think should be entitled to a share of this fortune.*

💡 *Choose the top three contenders who you think deserve the fortune.*

*On your own, think about who has the 'greatest claim' and who has the 'weakest claim' on this fortune. Jot down reasons for your judgement.*

💡 **Remember!**

*An old shipping law says that shipwrecks are the property of those who find and search them. Should a law be more important than anything else in deciding who has the 'greatest claim'?*

## The main contenders to the throne

Edward the Confessor named Harold Godwin as his successor on his deathbed in January 1066. While the Witan backed Edward's choice, at least three other men, William of Normandy, Prince Edgar the Atheling and Harold Hardrada, believed neither Edward nor the Witan had any power to make this decision and decided to fight against it. These men felt that they also had a claim on the English throne.

# TASKS...

**1** All four contenders claimed they were the rightful kings of England. Now it is time for you to choose which one was correct. You will need to do a SWOT analysis for each contender when you have read the information about that person. For each person, you need to copy into your book the chart below and fill in the details. Allow yourself plenty of room for the answers. **WS**

| Name of contender: | |
|---|---|
| **Strengths** | *Summarise the claims of the contender.* |
| **Weaknesses** | *Summarise why these claims might not be very strong.* |
| **Opportunities** | *Summarise how or why he might be able to achieve his ambition to be king.* |
| **Threats** | *Summarise the dangers the contender might face if he tries to gain the English throne.* |

# William of Normandy

William's family were descendants of Vikings who had settled in northern France at the beginning of the tenth century. When his father died on a **pilgrimage** to the Holy Land in 1035 (he was probably murdered), William was named as his successor as Duke of Normandy at the age of just 8.

**William the Conqueror.**

William faced many threats to his rule and it was not until 1063 that he finally felt safe in power. During this time he built a reputation for acts of cruelty, and a love of money and power. William did not lose a single battle or fail to capture a castle. Like Hardrada and Godwin, his reputation as a military genius was well known.

William claimed the English throne on several counts. First, he was related to the kings of England. His grand aunt (Emma) had married both King Ethelred and King Canute. This meant William was related to both Edward the Confessor and Harthacanute.

William also claimed that in 1051 Edward the Confessor invited him to London and had named him as his successor. In addition, William claimed that in 1064 Harold swore an oath over the Bible and the **relics** of Saint-Valery that he would support William's claim to the throne when Edward died. In those days people believed you would burn in hell forever if you broke a **sacred** oath!

In order to make his claim for the throne, William had to launch an invasion of England in 1066. Luckily, his neighbours around Normandy were either too weak or too distracted to try invading Normandy while he was away. This meant he could concentrate on invading England.

### Key words

**Pilgrimage** A journey to a holy place.

**Relics** The bones of an important person, or something that belonged to that person.

**Sacred** Something that is very holy and special.

**Cavalry** The part of an army that fights on horseback.

The Normans were known for having the best **cavalry** in Europe. They bred horses that were tall and fast. William's soldiers trained for long periods of time. Their skills as archers and bowmen were equal to any army in Europe. William had about 30,000 trained soldiers to help him fight. But the Normans did have one major weakness – their navy. They didn't have much knowledge or skills in this area.

Edgar Atheling.

Harald Hardrada.

## Prince Edgar the Atheling

Very little is known about Prince Edgar. He was just fourteen years old when his great uncle, King Edward the Confessor, died. We do know that Edgar was Edward's nearest blood relative. Edward and Edgar were both descendants of King Ethelred. Edgar's grandfather, Edmund Ironside, had ruled England briefly in 1016.

In 1057, Edward the Confessor clearly and publicly named Edgar's father, Edward the Atheling, as his successor. Both the Witan and Harold Godwin backed this decision. However, Edward the Atheling died mysteriously while visiting King Edward. Both Harold Godwin and William of Normandy are suspected of being involved in the murder.

Because Prince Edgar was only five when his father died and fourteen when Edward lay dying, few people thought he would be the next king. Edgar was obviously very young. He had little money, no soldiers and no experience of battle. As the English waited for attacks from Norway, Normandy, Scotland and Denmark, neither Edward the Confessor nor the Witan believed Prince Edgar was a sensible choice.

## Harald Hardrada

Harald was born in 1015 to the son of a nobleman who ruled a small part of Norway. In 1030, he fought unsuccessfully with his uncle, King Olaf of Norway, in a fierce civil war. Olaf was killed and Harald escaped to Sweden before travelling on to **Kiev**.

Between 1034 and 1043, Harald led the world-famous Varangian Guard. They were a ruthless army employed by the Byzantine Empire based in **Constantinople**. For nine years, Harald cleared the Aegean and Mediterranean seas of pirates. He fought battles in places like modern-day Israel, Africa and Sicily. He became the most famous and experienced warrior in the world.

Throughout these battles he collected a huge hoard of treasure, which he guarded fiercely.

Harald was ambitious. He wanted to be King of Norway. At first, he fought against King Magnus of Norway. Later, he ruled alongside him for one year. After Magnus died in 1047, Harald became the sole ruler.

King Magnus had been friendly with Harthacanute, a former King of England. Harthacanute had promised that, when he died, Magnus could have the English throne. However, when Harthacanute died in 1042, Magnus was too busy fighting the Danes to take the English crown. This meant that Edward the Confessor was able to step in and claim the throne for himself (see pages 12–14).

Most people, including Harald, had forgotten about Harthacanute's promise to King Magnus. All of that changed with the mysterious arrival of Tostig (Harold Godwin's brother) at Harald's court in Norway. Tostig and Harold Godwin had quarrelled, and Tostig had fled England to escape death. Once in Norway, Tostig reminded Harald of Harthacnut's promise to King Magnus. He also convinced Harald that the people of northern England hated Harold Godwin and wanted the Vikings to return. Gradually Harald began to develop plans to invade England and lay claim to the English throne.

## Key words

**Infantry** The part of an army that fights on foot.

Harald had between 12,000 and 18,000 soldiers who were ready to fight. He also had about 300 ships for the long sea voyage from Norway. Like the English, the Vikings preferred hand-to-hand combat to a cavalry. However, both **infantry** and horses could be taken if they were needed. England is a long way from Norway, and Harald's army would not be able to carry enough food with them to last through a war. He knew that they would have to rely on the kindness of English people as they passed through towns and villages, or to steal food.

Harold Godwin.

## Harold Godwin

Harold's family gained a lot of money and power during the reign of King Canute. Harold's father was made an earl in 1018, and by 1066 the family was the richest and most powerful in England. Harold owned almost the whole of the southern half of England. He was very popular with his own people.

From the late 1050s, the ageing King Edward completely relied on Harold to defend his kingdom. Edward's main threat came from the kings of Wales. After several bold attacks by Welsh armies, Harold joined up with his brother Tostig to defeat them in 1063.

Harold's sister, Edith, was married to King Edward. However, in the eleventh century, kingship was not **hereditary**. This meant that the eldest son of a king did not automatically become the next king. Anyone could be king if they were chosen by the Witan.

Harold had been named by King Edward as subregulus (deputy king). He was also seen as England's most able soldier and therefore the most suitable heir to the throne. As Edward was dying, he had said that the 46-year-old Harold should be the next king. In Anglo-Saxon culture, the dying wishes of a king were considered sacred.

### Key words

**Hereditary** Passed down through the family.

Harold's Anglo-Saxon warriors hardly ever fought on horseback. They preferred hand-to-hand combat with axes. In fact, the Englishman's skill with an axe is thought to have put off many armies from invading. The English were also good sailors. A large navy patrolled the waters around the English Channel and the North Sea. Given enough warning and time, Harold could have called on an army of 10,000 trained soldiers and up to 240,000 untrained peasants to fight.

# TASKS...

1  Using the results of your SWOT analysis, which person do you think had the strongest claim to the throne?

2  **a)**  Now consider the factors below. Make a chart in your book like the one here, and rate each contender on a scale of 1 to 10. **WS**

|  | William | Edgar | Harald Hardrada | Harold Godwin |
|---|---|---|---|---|
| Blood relation<br>Experience of warfare<br>Popular among the English<br>Well trained army<br>Good tactics<br>Right to the English throne | | | | |
| Totals | | | | |

   **b)**  Which of the six factors listed in your chart do you think should be the most important in deciding who should be king?

3  Compare the results of your SWOT analysis with the scores in the chart. Has your opinion changed about which person had the strongest claim to the throne? Who do you think has the strongest vote? Take a class vote. Does the whole class agree on the same person?

## Plenary

The SWOT analysis is a useful way of analysing situations.

Which other situations could you use a SWOT analysis for?

Perform a SWOT analysis on another situation, either from a different lesson or from your own life. For example, you could use a SWOT analysis to consider fox hunting, capital punishment, going to war, choosing a new home or car, or deciding where to go on holiday.

# THE ALLEGED OATHS: DID HE OR DIDN'T HE?

By the end of this section you will be able to answer these questions.
- Did Harold really swear an oath to support William?
- Why can't we be sure about what really happened in 1064?
- Why was Harold's oath so important to the Normans?

You will also look at what makes a reliable source and what makes a misleading one.

## Starter

*Look at Source A.*

**A witness in the stand in a modern-day court of law. Notice how her right hand is holding a copy of the Bible. She is about to take an oath: 'I swear to tell the truth, the whole truth, and nothing but the truth, so help me God.'**

💡 *What is an 'oath'?*

💡 *Why do you think witnesses swear an oath before they are questioned by the court?*

💡 *Why do you think many people are afraid of telling lies after they have sworn an oath to God?*

💡 *What do you think might happen to a witness if he or she tells lies? Who might punish the witness for lying?*

## The sacred oath

Back in the eleventh century almost everybody believed in God. As you will see in Chapter 4, people in England believed in a Christian God. They also believed that when you died you would find either eternal paradise in heaven or eternal suffering in hell.

One of the surest ways to go to hell was to break a sacred oath – that is, to make a promise to God that you didn't keep. People believed that if you broke a sacred oath, your honour and soul would be destroyed forever.

William of Normandy had told the **Pope** that both Edward the Confessor and Harold Godwin promised to support his claim to the throne. The Pope believed William and publically supported his claim. But did Edward and Harold really make these promises? If not, did William deserve the English throne?

Look at the storyboard here and on the next page to examine *the Norman version of events*. **WS**

*Edward loved the Normans. After all, his mother was Norman and the Normans had protected him as a child. During Edward's exile in Normandy, he grew to love and admire the young William. They became great friends.*

*In 1051, King Edward turned his thoughts to who would succeed him. Edward's love of Normandy led him to choose William as his heir. Edward invited William to London and offered him the crown of England when he died. Edward and all the Earls of England, including Godwin, swore an oath of loyalty to William and his right to the throne.*

*William returned to Normandy and waited patiently for the death of the old king. In 1064, Edward sent his most trusted **ally**, Harold Godwin, to Normandy. He wanted to reassure William that he hadn't changed his mind.*

As Harold sailed to Normandy, a sudden and violent storm shipwrecked his fleet. Everyone apart from Harold drowned. A lighthouse keeper saved Harold. He fed and clothed him, and took him to William for safe keeping.

Harold passed on Edward's message. He also swore a sacred oath to support William's claim to the throne. Harold spent several months in Normandy, fighting and hunting alongside William. They became great friends.

💡 Which aspects of the story appear likely? Which appear unlikely?

## Did Harold really make the oath?

### Key words

**Alleged** Something someone is supposed to have said or done, but that hasn't actually been proven.

No one who fought on the battlefield at Hastings or who was closely involved in the **alleged** oath by Harold wrote a single word about the events leading up to and including 1066. Most accounts were written in the years after 1066. We cannot be sure where people at the time got their information. We cannot be certain whether Harold made an oath at all. Even if Harold did swear an oath, we cannot be sure exactly what he promised to do.

# TASKS...

You are going to write a structured account based on the information in this section. Answers to questions 1 to 6 will help you with this piece of writing. **WS**

**1** What did people in the Middle Ages think would happen if you broke a sacred oath?

**2** Why do you think Harold may have been in Normandy in 1064?

**3** What evidence is there that Harold *did* swear an oath in Normandy?

**4** What evidence is there that Harold *did not* swear an oath in Normandy?

**5** Find reasons why we cannot trust the Normans' version of events.

**6** Find reasons why an oath by Harold may not have counted in any case.

**7** Use your answers to questions 1 to 6 to write an extended answer to the following question.
*'Did Harold Godwin swear an oath in support of William in 1064?'*
Here is some advice to help you to write a good answer.

### Introduction
You should write about the argument you are going to make in your answer. Explain why the oath was so important to the Normans.

### First paragraph
Write about the evidence that suggests Harold did make an oath in 1064.

> **TIP!**
> Each paragraph should have an attention-grabbing topic sentence!

### Second paragraph
Write about why we should be suspicious of the Norman evidence about this oath. Why do many historians doubt such an oath took place? This would be a good chance to use the other explanations as to why Harold might have been in Normandy at this time.

### Conclusion
You could comment on whether we should accept the Normans' claims about this oath. You could also include some of the reasons why an oath might not have counted anyway.

---

## Plenary

**Reliability** is important when using historical sources.  Considering all the information in this section, how reliable do you think an oath is?

Can an oath *ever* be reliable?

# HOW DID EACH LEADER PREPARE FOR WAR IN 1066?

**Objectives**

By the end of this section you will be aware of:
- what might have been going through the minds of Harold, William and Harald in early 1066.

You will understand the answers to these questions:
- Which of the three had the strongest army?
- Why did all three contenders believe they could win the throne?

## Starter

### *Decisions, decisions …*

*Imagine you are going on a long voyage of discovery to the Arctic Circle. Your adventure will last about four weeks. You can only take five items from the list below.*

| tent | sleeping bag | gun/bullets | water | chocolate |
| --- | --- | --- | --- | --- |
| dried food | gas stove | skis | sun cream | gloves/hat |
| binoculars | camera | mobile phone | sunglasses | first aid kit |

*Which items should you choose? On your own choose:*

- *5 essentials*    ● *5 desirables*    ● *5 luxuries*

*Now share your decisions with other class members. Are your decisions the same? If they are different, why are they different?*

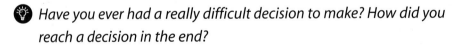 *Have you ever had a really difficult decision to make? How did you reach a decision in the end?*

## Who would become king?

As we have seen on pages 18–22, there were four contenders to the English throne – Prince Edgar, Harald Hardrada, William of Normandy and Harold Godwin.

Edgar, who was only fourteen, was unable to challenge Harold. The other three contenders must have thought long and hard about whether they should try to become king. Harald, William and Harold all had the right experience and power to become king. Look at what each man might have thought about his challenge to the throne.

## Key words

**Housecarls** Warriors.

**Halley's comet** A comet that appears about every 76 years above the earth's skies.

💡 For all 3 contenders, which thoughts are *for* challenging the throne, and which are *against* challenging the throne?

### What Harald Hardrada might have thought …

The people of northern England hate Harold Godwin anyway and would welcome another Viking king.

English **housecarls** are the most feared in all the world.

It is a dangerous journey to England. How will I get all my men, horses and supplies there safely?

When I win, I will be known as one of the greatest warriors in the history of the world.

I will become the richest man in the world.

I can't be sure the people of northern England will welcome me.

Godwin will probably be destroyed by William in the south, leaving northern England undefended.

What if Godwin beats William's men, then turns his whole army against us?

### What William of Normandy might have thought …

Unless we win quickly we won't have enough supplies.

Norman cavalry, archers and infantry are very skilful.

Good omens like **Halley's comet** and the support of Pope Alexander II prove that God is on our side.

The English people see me as a foreigner. They will never accept me as their new ruler.

I might not get safely across the English Channel.

I have never lost a battle in my whole life.

Godwin's forces are spread too thinly across England. I can destroy his armies one by one.

Godwin is a great and popular warrior. He might beat me.

## What Harold Godwin might have thought …

> Both Harald and William will struggle to bring enough men across the seas to England.

> If we are not attacked before September, we will have to send home most of our army to collect in the harvests.

> The Normans will be unable to bring enough food and supplies to last them more than a few weeks.

> Although I have a much bigger army, William's army is better trained.

> I might have to fight two invaders at the same time.

> I can't trust powerful nobles like Earl Edwin of Mercia and Earl Morcar of Northumbria to support me. They would do anything to win their independence.

> If I sail the navy along the south coast, I might destroy the Normans before they even step foot on English soil.

> As long as I am alive, the southern English will fight to the death for me.

# TASKS…

1. Get into groups of three. Each person in the group should pretend to be either Harald, William or Harold. Read through that person's thoughts again and become an expert on your contender's **dilemma** in 1066. It might help to go back and remind yourself of their claims to the throne (see pages 18–22).

2. Still in your groups, interview each other by putting 'Harald', 'William' and then 'Harold' in the hot seat. It might help to ask some of these questions.

- Why do you think you should be king in the first place? (See pages 18–22.)
- What makes you think you can win a war?
- What doubts or worries do you have?
- Name one factor that the success of your army depends on.

### Key words

**Dilemma** A difficult choice or decision.

# Who had the strongest army?

## The English

The armour, helmets, spears and swords of the English and the Normans were all similar. But the soldiers looked very different on the battlefield.

**A member of the English fyrd.**

Harold's army was made up of a small group known as the housecarls and a much larger group known as the **fyrd**. The housecarls were fully trained professional soldiers. The fyrd were less experienced and less well equipped. At the Battle of Hastings, Harold led 500 housecarls and 7000 fyrd. The housecarls would have ridden into battle on horses. But they preferred to fight on foot.

Only the housecarls and a small number of the fyrd could afford a **hauberk**, which provided some protection in battle. Unlike the Normans, the English preferred to use the battle-axe. Also unlike the Normans, the English had few archers or slingshots among their ranks. The English preferred hand-to-hand combat.

**An English housecarl.**

## The Normans

The army that William brought with him to England was 7500 men strong. About 4000 or 5000 more people accompanied the soldiers as blacksmiths, carpenters, medics and cooks. All of the soldiers were fully trained, like Harold's housecarls. In addition, there were an unknown number (maybe 500) of **mercenaries** who, like all the other soldiers, were promised payment and booty if William won.

**A Norman infantry man.**

The infantry carried at least two weapons. The first was a twin-edged 'slashing sword' about one metre in length. The second was a javelin or spear, about two metres in length, made of ash wood with a sharp iron tip.

It is likely that the only sections of William's army without armour were his archers and slingshots. Their arrows could kill a man about 100 metres away, if the arrow or pebble was accurately fired.

**A Norman cavalryman.**

### The Norwegians

**A Norwegian Viking.**

We know very little about what Harald Hardrada's soldiers looked like as they journeyed into battle. Historians have estimated that between 12,000 and 18,000 men left Norway with Hardrada.

As Vikings, the Norwegians traditionally attacked from the sea and did not rely on horses in battle. Hand-to-hand combat was their favourite method of fighting. In that sense they were very similar in appearance and tactics to the English.

## TASKS...

**1 a)** In pairs, choose either the English (Harold's men), Normans (William's men) or Norwegians (Harald's men) to investigate in full. Read the text on pages 31–2. Then give scores out of 10 and explanations for each aspect of their armies. Draw charts like the one below. Remember to give yourself enough space to write. **WS**

| Army under investigation: | | | |
|---|---|---|---|
| | Score out of 10 | Advantages | Disadvantages |
| Armour | | | |
| Weapons | | | |
| Cavalry | | | |
| Archers and bowmen | | | |
| Training | | | |

**b)** Who do you think had the strongest army? Now look back to the SWOT analyses you did on pages 19–22. Do these give the same answer?

**2 a)** Look at the adjectives in the word grid below. Some of these words might be used to describe the three main contenders – Harald Hardrada, William of Normandy and Harold Godwin.

| daring | adventurous | unlucky | wealthy | cunning |
|---|---|---|---|---|
| deceptive | wise | organised | rash | foolish |
| trusting | ill-prepared | confident | unwise | lucky |

# TASKS...

**b)** Choose two words from the grid to describe Harold's plans and preparations for battle. Give explanations for your choice. Now do the same for Harald and William.

**c)** Discuss your choices with your neighbour or the class. Do you all have the same opinion of these men?

## Plenary

Think about the armies of Harald, William and Harold. Which army would have preferred:

- a surprise attack
- a pre-arranged battle
- a series of battles over a few days?

Be prepared to justify your choices.

# HOW DID THE FIGHTING START AT FULFORD GATE, STAMFORD BRIDGE AND HASTINGS?

**Objectives**

By the end of this section you will be able to answer the following questions.
- Who came out best by the end of 1066 – Harald Hardrada, Harold Godwin or William the Conqueror?
- Was luck the most decisive factor in the battles of 1066?

You will analyse Harold's decisions.

## Starter

# ENGLAND 6 : BRAZIL 0

Imagine this is the final score of the next Football World Cup final. It is a victory that few English people can imagine – nevertheless, many strange things can happen – especially in History. If you were to investigate the causes of this footballing victory, you might be able to split them into three categories.

*Make a chart in your book like the one below. Then read the following statements. Put these statements into the most appropriate column.*

*a) Brazil's star player broke his leg in the semi-final.*

*b) The Brazilian manager risked his seventeen year-old second-choice goalkeeper.*

*c) The England manager decided on a traditional 4-4-2 formation.*

*d) The Brazilian captain kept urging his players to go forward and defend less.*

*e) All of England's best players were 100 per cent fit.*

*f) The England players had practised winning the ball and counter-attacking.*

*This activity will help you later on when we analyse the events of the Battle of Hastings and try to answer the big question, 'Did Harold deserve to lose the Battle of Hastings?'*

| Good luck | Good decisions by England | Bad decisions by Brazil |
|---|---|---|
| This is when victory occurs because one side seems to have everything going in its favour. | This is when victory occurs because of good decisions or planning. | This is when victory occurs because the opponent makes errors or mistakes. |
| Examples | Examples | Examples |
| 1. | 1. | 1. |
| 2. | 2. | 2. |

# Preparations for war

Wars and battles are very similar to games of football. When one side wins it is usually because it has been lucky and has made lots of good decisions. It also helps when the enemy has made a series of bad decisions! The following sections tell you about the battles that took place in 1066. Each section (including this one) has some questions. As you read, you should answer these questions in your book. Your answers need not be in full sentences. Instead, try to use keywords, names and dates.

### *Getting ready*

In late spring 1066, Harold Godwin and the English were expecting Harald Hardrada and William of Normandy to make an attack at any time. In February, William had brought together his leading nobles to discuss battle plans. Spies had told Harold Godwin that Harald Hardrada and William were busy making preparations for their invasions and, in late April, Harold called up an army of 50,000 men.

The English expected William to attack first. However, by late August nothing had happened. Harold Godwin now suspected that Harald Hardrada would attack in September or even October. But he had begun to think that William would not launch his attack at all that year. As a result, Harold let his fyrd army go home in early September to collect the harvest.

Meanwhile, William's army was ready to attack in Normandy, but didn't leave until the middle of September. William's two thousand boats were very fragile. He had to avoid even the calmest storm if his army were to cross the English Channel safely. During this delay most of the English navy had been destroyed in a storm. Also, because the fyrd was collecting in the harvest, the south of England was badly defended.

- Which of the three contenders do you think took the biggest risk?

- Do you think William's delayed departure was a wise decision or simply good luck for William?

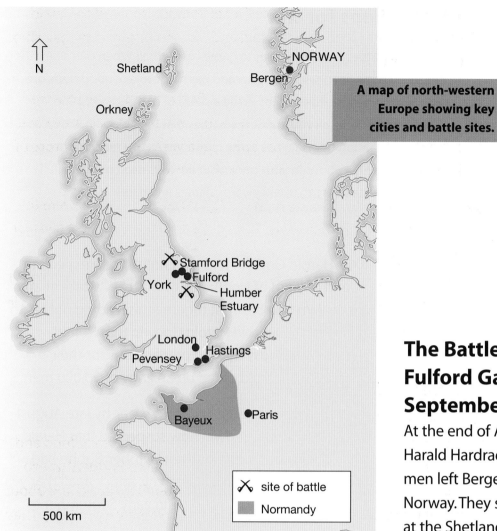

A map of north-western Europe showing key cities and battle sites.

Labels on map: N, Shetland, Orkney, NORWAY, Bergen, Stamford Bridge, Fulford, York, Humber Estuary, London, Hastings, Pevensey, Bayeux, Paris

Legend:
✗ site of battle
Normandy

500 km

## The Battle of Fulford Gate, 20 September 1066

At the end of August 1066, Harald Hardrada and his men left Bergen, in Norway. They stopped off at the Shetland and Orkney Islands, then sailed down the east coast of Scotland. Coastal towns and villages were attacked and raided for food and water before Harald Hardrada's ships finally began sailing along the River Humber. Harald's goal was to capture the City of York. Unfortunately for him, word of these attacks was passed by spies to Harold Godwin in the south of England in early September. Harold called the English army for a second time; Harald Hardrada could no longer take the English army by surprise!

Harald's army of about 6000 men left their ships safely anchored at Riccall and began the march towards York. On 20 September, Harald finally met some English resistance about a kilometre from York. Edwin and Morcar (the Earls of Mercia and Northumbria) confronted Harald and blocked his path at Fulford Gate. A 30-minute fight ended with Harald winning the first battle of 1066.

Four days later (24 September), the City of York surrendered to Harald without a fight. Following this, Harald and his men returned to their ships in Riccall to rest and celebrate their victory.

Harald Hardrada didn't know that Harold Godwin and his men were already on their way north to deal with the invaders. Harald may have calculated that Harold would not arrive for a week after the capture of York – plenty of time to relax and create a battle strategy.

- 💡 Why do you think Harald's men needed to raid coastal towns and villages?

- 💡 How do you think Harald felt after the victories at Fulford Gate and York?

- 💡 What do you think were the advantages of these raids for Harold Godwin?

- 💡 Why do you think Harald and his men returned to their ships in Riccall?

## The Battle of Stamford Bridge, 25 September 1066

Harald ordered the people of York to hand over their livestock, food and gold. The hand-over was due to take place at Stamford Bridge, thirteen kilometres from York. On the morning of 25 September, Harald and about a third of his men set off to collect their goods. It was a very hot day. They left all their armour on board the ships and carried only swords.

As Harald and his men collected their cattle and grain, the sound of galloping English horses filled the air. Harald had not bothered to position watchmen and was therefore shocked to discover that Harold's army had arrived several days earlier than expected.

Harold Godwin rode up boldly to Harald Hardrada and his brother Tostig. Tostig turned down Harold's offer of a **pardon** and land in return for switching sides. Harold returned to his men and the battle began. We do not know how many Englishmen fought Harald's 5000 men. However, by late afternoon, Tostig had been slaughtered and Harald had suffered a fatal arrow wound to his throat.

### Key words

**Pardon** An official statement of forgiveness.

A modern painting of the Battle of Stamford Bridge in 1066.

Despite Harold's offers of a safe journey back to Norway, Harald Hardrada's men fought on in vain. Although they knew that they could never win, they fought on to protect their honour and their fallen king.

Harold Godwin's men also had to face the rest of Harald's army, which had arrived from Riccall after Harald's death. An exhausted English army was therefore forced to fight another three or four hours of hand-to-hand combat. By nightfall the English had finally slaughtered most of Harald Hardrada's army. It was the last time that either the Norwegians or the Vikings threatened the shores of Europe – such was the scale of Harald's defeat and Harold Godwin's victory.

# TASKS...

1 Write a commentary on the Battle of Stamford Bridge in the style of a football commentator. Say who made good and bad decisions, and who had the lucky breaks.

💡 Why do you think Harald travelled with so few men and armour to Stamford Bridge?

💡 What do you think we can learn about Harald from this decision?

💡 How do you think this last brave stand by Harald's men might have helped William of Normandy?

# The Battle of Hastings, 14 October 1066

According to legend, Harold and his men feasted and drank all night to celebrate their spectacular victory at Stamford Bridge. After all, Harald Hardrada was seen as the greatest soldier in the world. The next morning, Harold called a council to discuss what to do next. At this point neither Harold nor his men had any idea if William had already landed in southern England.

💡 Should Harold have waited and rested for a few weeks? Or should he have marched south immediately to face William? Explain why you think this.

### Three decisions

Harold made three decisions that were to have a huge effect on the history of England.

| ONE | TWO | THREE |
|---|---|---|
| He told his fyrd army that they would not receive any gold until William had been beaten as well. | He did not allow Edwin and Morcar to regain their control of Northumbria. Instead he appointed a new 'sheriff' called Meruleswegen to rule when he was not there. | He decided to ride at full speed towards the south coast with his housecarls. He also ordered the fyrd and his archers to rest for two days, then to follow on foot and meet him in London. |

# TASKS...

1 In pairs, look at Harold's three decisions. *Think very hard* about the effects each decision might have. List one or two *good* things and one or two *bad* things about each decision.

For example, for decision One, a good thing might be that the army would fight hard so that they would get the gold. A bad thing for decision One might be that the army may decide to run away and not fight.

2 What advice would you have given Harold about the three decisions?

### Tactics

On 26 September 1066, Harold and 200 housecarls began their week-long ride towards London. The very next evening, William and his men set sail from Normandy. They landed near Pevensey before midday on 28 September. To William's relief, the whole area was completely deserted. Harold had guessed wrongly that William would invade Dover and had only left troops there.

William ordered a wooden castle to be built in Pevensey, then forced the people of nearby Hastings to provide his men with livestock and food. Meanwhile, William's men attacked English farms, stealing livestock and burning down homes.

On 6 October, Harold Godwin and his housecarls arrived in London after a 320-kilometre journey that had taken them eight days. They already knew about William's arrival. Harold called another council to decide what to do next. He had two options.

**OPTION 1:
I could attack William immediately.**

**OPTION 2:
I could attack William later.**

This tactic had defeated Hardrada just two weeks earlier. Although Harold had 200 housecarls, his fyrd army had not yet caught up with him so he would have to call a whole new army to face William. However, he may have thought not all of William's army had arrived, which meant they could be caught before they were ready.

This idea came from Harold's younger brother Gyrth. He suggested that Harold should wait for the northern fyrd and archers to arrive, which meant they would be better prepared to attack William. Gyrth pointed out that they could outnumber the Normans by three or four to one – if they waited. He argued that William's huge army would soon run out of food and therefore be easier to beat. Others disagreed, saying that William's reinforcements were growing daily and that supplies were arriving from Normandy all the time.

💡 What would you have done if you were Harold?

💡 What do you think William was hoping Harold would decide?

### The attack

In the end, Harold decided not to wait. Instead, he launched an immediate attack on William's forces. Harold called in another fyrd from the counties of southern England to face William. The brand new army was forced to march quickly from London towards Hastings, a distance of 96 kilometres, in just three days. Shortly after midnight on 14 October 1066, Harold's men arrived on the fields where the Battle of Hastings would take place just hours later. Unlike Harald Hardrada, William had positioned watchmen who told him of Harold's midnight arrival.

## TASKS...

1 Imagine you are one of Harold's housecarls. Most housecarls go into battle with their wives at their sides. The wives watch the battle from a nearby hill. If their husbands die, they bury them. On this occasion, your wife cannot come with you. Make notes for her about the last few weeks. The questions below will help.

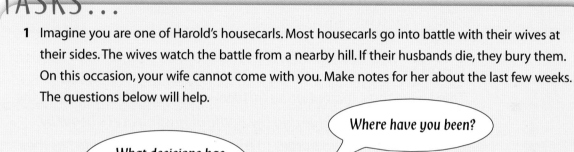

Where have you been?

What decisions has Harold made?

What have you seen and done?

Do you think you will beat William, and why?

Do you still believe Harold is a wise leader?

2 Do you think Harold was destined to lose the battle against William before it even began? Explain your answer.

## Plenary

List five factors that were important in deciding the outcome of the battles of Fulford Gate and Stamford Bridge.

Now rank these five factors in order. What was the most important factor for each battle?

Was it mainly luck or good decision-making that led to the victories at Fulford Gate and Stamford Bridge?

# DID HAROLD DESERVE TO LOSE THE ENGLISH THRONE?

**Objectives**

You will look at what we have learned so far in this section that might help us answer the key question:

• Did Harold deserve to be defeated at the Battle of Hastings?

You will also look at:

• how debate can help us to listen to other's views and learn new ideas

• how we can persuade other people to change their opinions.

## Starter

*There were three major battles in 1066 – the Battle of Fulford Gate, the Battle of Stamford Bridge and the Battle of Hastings. Let's begin by analysing the first two battles to try to decide why they ended as they did. Brainstorm in pairs why you think each person won that battle.*

| The Battle of Fulford Gate | |
|---|---|
| **Victor** | Harald Hardrada and the Norwegian Vikings |
| **Defeated** | The Northern English led by Earls Edwin and Morcar |
| **Date** | 20 September 1066 |
| **Location** | Fulford, near York |

| The Battle of Stamford Bridge | |
|---|---|
| **Victor** | Harold Godwin and the English |
| **Defeated** | Harald Hardrada, Tostig and the Norwegian Vikings |
| **Date** | 25 September 1066 |
| **Location** | Stamford Bridge, north east of York |

*For each battle create a table like the one below. Fill in as much information as you can for the three categories for both Harold Godwin and Harald Hardrada at each of the battles. Look back at page 34 to see how you did this for the football match.*

| Good luck | Good decisions | Bad decisions |
|---|---|---|
| | | |

## Defeat for Harold

The Battle of Hastings began on the morning of 14 October 1066. It lasted all day. The timeline, map and Sources A to D record the key events of the battle.

## TIMELINE
### The Battle of Hastings, 14 October 1066

**2.30 am** Harold cancels his plan to attack the Normans at night after a Norman watchman spots them.

**7 am** Harold positions English troops at the top of Senlac Hill.

**11 am** The Normans send in their infantry. They are quickly cut down by English axes, swords and spears. The English defensive wall holds up well against the Norman cavalry, who struggle up Senlac Hill.

**12.30 pm** As part of the Norman cavalry retreat, a small number of the English fyrd chase after them before returning to their lines. Had William now learned a way of drawing the English from their hill top position?

**1.30 pm** In the middle of a successful English counter-attack on the Normans, Harold's brother, Leofwine, is killed. Harold orders his men to return to the top of Senlac Hill. Thirty minutes later, Harold's brother, Gyrth, is killed.

**4.30 pm** William's cavalry successfully attacks the fyrd on Harold's right wing. Many in the fyrd fear defeat and run away. The English are soon outnumbered and the Normans get closer.

**5.15 pm** The housecarls form a defensive wall around Harold. One by one they die, until Harold himself is killed. Not a single housecarl is left alive by nightfall.

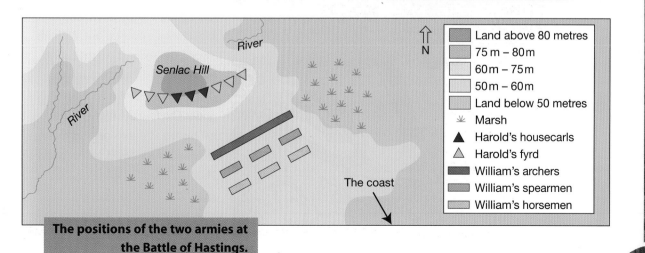

**The positions of the two armies at the Battle of Hastings.**

Our soldiers attacked, hurling spears at the English. They resisted bravely and returned the fire with spears, axes and stones. Our knights crashed into the enemy shields but the English remained on high ground, keeping close order, and pushed our knights down the hill.

Our knights remembered the trick of retreating and pretending to flee. Several thousand English quickly chased them down the hill. Once down the hill, the Normans suddenly turned their horses, surrounded the enemy and cut them down. Twice this trick was employed, and at last the English were defeated.

**From a description by William of Poitiers, a Norman who was not at the battle but who later became one of William's most trusted officials.**

SOURCE B

William took Harold by surprise before his men were ready to fight. The English army had a very small space; and many soldiers saw this difficult position and deserted King Harold. Even so, he fought bravely and the enemy's army made little impression on him until, after great killing on both sides, the king fell.

**Extract from the *Anglo-Saxon Chronicle*, written by English monks, which recorded an English view of what happened at the Battle of Hastings.**

SOURCE C

**A scene from the Bayeux Tapestry showing Harold being killed (by an arrow in the eye). The Bayeux Tapestry is an embroidered illustration of the Norman conquest of England.**

SOURCE D

With the point of the lance, the first knight pierced Harold's shield and then penetrated his chest, drenching the ground with his blood which poured out. With his sword, the second knight cut off Harold's head. The third knight disembowelled him with his spear. The fourth knight hacked off his leg at the thigh and threw it away. Struck down in this way, Harold's dead body lay on the ground.

**Extract from a poem written in about 1068 by a Norman bishop.**

By dusk, Harold and his army had been completely destroyed by the Normans. Harold's army was in full retreat and Harold lay dead. On 25 December 1066, William of Normandy was crowned King of England in London.

# TASKS...

1 In groups, answer the following questions.
   a) Do you think Harold missed any opportunities to win the Battle of Hastings?
   b) Do you think William would have won if Harold had more archers and reinforcements?
   c) Why do you think that Sources A to D give different accounts of what happened at the Battle of Hastings?

2 Now analyse the Battle of Hastings to try to decide why it ended as it did, filling in the table below to indicate good luck and good decisions for William, and bad decisions for Harold. In pairs, brainstorm why you think each person won that battle.

| Good luck | Good decisions | Bad decisions |
|-----------|----------------|---------------|
|           |                |               |

3 Now that we have come to the end of our investigation, we must reach some conclusions. Start with a revision game to see how much information you have remembered from the whole of this chapter. Look at the chart below. For each of the seven rows, work out which person, thing or event is the odd one out. Share your views with a neighbour, and then with the whole class.

| | | | | | |
|---|---|---|---|---|---|
| 1 | King Edward | Prince Edgar | Harold Godwin | Harald Hardrada | William of Normandy |
| 2 | Harthacanute | William of Normandy | Emma | Ethelred | Harefoot |
| 3 | slingshot | canons | bow and arrow | warhorses | axes |
| 4 | York | Stamford Bridge | Hastings | Fulford | Pevensey |
| 5 | William of Normandy | Harold Godwin | Edward the Confessor | Harald Hardrada | Tostig |
| 6 | shipwrecked | sent by King Edward | wanted to free hostages | meeting European leaders | spying mission |
| 7 | Romans | Nazis | Celts | Normans | Vikings |

## EXTENSION TASK …

**4** As a class, debate the question: *Did Harold deserve to lose the English throne?*
A good debate on this should tackle the following questions. ◆**WS**

- *Whose claim to the throne was the greater – Harold's or William's?*

- *Whose army was the more powerful – Harold's or William's?*

- *Who made the best and worst decisions – Harold or William?*

- *Who was luckier – Harold or William?*

## Plenary

History is all about what happened in the past. However, sometimes it can be useful to think about some 'What if …?' questions. As a class, discuss the list of questions below.

💡 *What if* Hardrada had not bothered to invade?

💡 *What if* Harold had accepted William as king and stood back as William and Hardrada fought one another instead?

💡 *What if* Harold had escaped the battlefield at Hastings?

💡 *What if* Hardrada had won the Battle of Stamford Bridge?

💡 *What if* William's navy had been sunk by Harold's navy in the English Channel?

See if you can add any more 'What if …?' questions to this list.

Even though we cannot change History, we can use these 'What if …?' questions to consider the huge impact of single decisions or events. Today England would be a very different place if either Harald Hardrada or Harold Godwin had won. It is easy to criticise someone in history with the benefit of hindsight. But try to identify one decision Harold Godwin and Harald Hardrada should have made that would have led to their victory in 1066.

# DID WILLIAM'S CONQUEST CHANGE ENGLAND?

*William was a Frenchman who had just become King of England. What problems do you think he would face as a king in a foreign country? Try to think of five.*

*Now rank these problems in order, starting with the most serious at the top and ending with the least serious at the bottom.*

*How would you have dealt with each of these problems if you had been William in 1066?*

## TIMELINE

**1066** Harold Godwin dies. William of Normandy is crowned King of England.

**1070** By now, William had defeated rebellions in Kent, Exeter, Durham and York.

**1072** Scotland's armies, led by Malcolm, King of Scots, surrender to William.

**1075** William defeats further rebellions in East Anglia and Hereford. He now controls most of England.

**1080** By now, nearly all the English bishops in the Church have been replaced by French bishops.

**1086** The 'Domesday Survey' is carried out.

**1087** William dies in France.

## What happened after 1066?

In Chapter 1, you read about the important events of 1066. You found out how William of Normandy defeated the English, led by Harold Godwin. You also learned how Harold Godwin died in 1066.

In this chapter you will look at the years following Harold's death. After his victory, William gave his French supporters large areas of land in England as a reward. He also introduced a feudal system which set out the rights people had and what duties they had to do. He built castles and cathedrals, altering the English landscape. He made changes to the way churches were built and run, and he brought in new rules about the services held there.

Historians don't agree about how important the events of these years are. Some say that William's victory was a turning point in English history – everything that people knew and were familiar with was changed forever. Others say that the amount of change wasn't that great, and that it's an exaggeration to claim that William's changes transformed England.

How far do you think the Norman invasion changed life in England? When you have read this chapter, you should be able to make up your mind.

DID WILLIAM'S CONQUEST CHANGE ENGLAND?

# HOW IMPORTANT WAS HAROLD'S DEATH?

**Objectives**

By the end of this section you will be able to answer these questions.

- How did people react to the news of Harold Godwin's death?
- What might English people be asking in 1066 about their new king?

You will look at a story written from a particular point of view and identify clues.

## Starter

*Imagine it is a few days after the Battle of Hastings. You are an Englishman, and you are drinking with some friends in a tavern. A trader, who is also drinking in the tavern, says he was at Hastings on 15 October 1066 (the morning after the battle). He begins to tell you a sad tale. When you have heard the whole story, you will find clues to show that the trader supported Harold and that he did not like William.* **WS**

💡 *In pairs, pick out all the words and phrases in the trader's story that show he was on Harold's side, and didn't like William and the Normans.*

💡 *What questions would you like to ask the trader? Come up with at least three.*

*Now find someone else in the class who has three different questions. Explain to each other why you chose your questions.*

### What the trader said

The 15th was a crisp autumn morning. Everywhere I looked I saw the ruins of battle. Dead warriors with broken shields and battle-axes lay cold and stiff, covered in blood. Their faces showed the pain they had suffered in bravely trying to save our noble king. I began to think about our defeat. Did it mean we were now William's slaves? I helped people search among the dead for their loved ones. It was a terrible task.

Only hours before, these men had stood bravely on the ridge of Senlac Hill. Their shields were locked together to form a strong wall that defended them all day from the Norman attacks. Harold – our leader and king – tried to hold off the invasion by the evil Norman duke, William of Normandy. He had already defeated an attack in the north. But his battle against William had gone horribly wrong. I watched sadly as his family and loyal friends searched for his body. I did what I could to help.

As we searched, we heard many stories about how the noble Harold died. People said that our brave men had held off several Norman charges. As evening approached, and the Norman soldiers looked like they were getting tired, Harold was hit by an arrow. It went straight through his eye and into his brain. His loyal bodyguards gathered round to protect him. But there was little they could do to ease his pain. The Normans made one last charge. This time, they broke through our line, and Harold was trapped. With terrible cruelty, they chopped his body into pieces. The battle was over. Those men who couldn't run away were brutally slaughtered.

'Here! He lies here!' cried one woman. There Harold lay, recognisable by the tattoos that only his closest relatives could identify. I tell those of you who are gathered today in this tavern, these are dark days. What can we expect now that we are to be ruled by a foreign duke? What must we English do about these events?

# TASKS...

1 Make a list of any *new* things you have found out about the Norman Conquest.

2 Some historians think the Norman invasion was a turning point in English history. Write a short paragraph on what you think about this view. When you have finished Chapter 2, check your paragraph again and see whether there is anything in it you would like to change.

## Plenary

Imagine you are one of Harold's relatives who helped discover his body in 1066. How would you want the English people to remember him?

Write an inscription of no more than 30 words to be carved on Harold's headstone. Bear in mind all the important events of the last two to three years.

# HOW MUCH DID THE ENGLISH TRY TO STOP THE NORMAN INVASION?

By the end of this section you will be able to answer these questions.

- How much opposition did the new king face?
- What evidence do we have about the rebels who opposed William after 1066?
- How did William deal with his opponents?

You will use the sources to decide whether evidence about this time is accurate and complete.

## Starter

*Look at Source A. Now look at the word grid below it. Pick out the adjectives you think describe the way the people in Source A must have been feeling at the time.*

SOURCE A

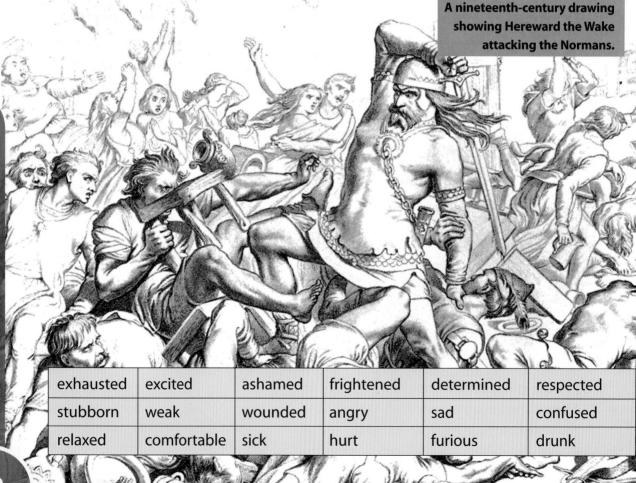

**A nineteenth-century drawing showing Hereward the Wake attacking the Normans.**

| exhausted | excited | ashamed | frightened | determined | respected |
| stubborn | weak | wounded | angry | sad | confused |
| relaxed | comfortable | sick | hurt | furious | drunk |

*Interpreting pictures and other visual sources is an important skill in history. Look at Source A again. Imagine you are the man wearing the helmet in the centre of the picture. Describe in your own words who you are and what you are doing. How do you feel? Why are you attacking the people in the picture?*

💡 *Why do you think Hereward was called 'the Wake'?*

💡 *What do you think this tells us about his character?*

## The rebellion of Hereward the Wake

A map showing William's control over different parts of Britain at different times in his reign.

The man in the centre of Source A with a sword over his shoulder is Hereward the Wake. In 1070, Hereward led a rebellion against the new king, William. By this time, people had already tried many times to remove William. Hereward had joined forces with Edwin (the Earl of Mercia), Morcar (the Earl of Northumberland) and an army of Danes. They based themselves on the island of Ely, an area in the Fens surrounded by marshland and water. Hereward and his supporters fought off the Normans for a year. But they were eventually defeated when William found a way of crossing the Fens.

There are many romantic stories about Hereward the Wake that tell of his strength, courage and fighting skill. Source A was drawn in the nineteenth century. It shows Hereward taking revenge on the Normans, who had invaded his home. Source B tells of how Hereward visited William's court disguised as a potter, when some drunken servants attacked him.

So snatching a piece of wood from the fireplace, he defended himself against them all, killing one of them and wounding many. [He was taken prisoner, but managed to escape on horseback to Ely.] One other pursuer fell into Hereward's hands. He was sent back to William by Hereward to tell the truth about what had happened. Everybody listened in amazement, and the king declared that Hereward was a generous and most remarkable knight.

**From *Gesta Herewardi*, composed by a monk at Ely some time in the twelfth century. The account is based on stories about Hereward, which are said to have been passed on by eyewitnesses.**

## The rebellion of Gytha

Another rebellion against William was led by Gytha, Harold Godwin's mother. It took place in 1068 in Exeter, Devon, which is where the Godwin family had a home.

After Harold's defeat at the Battle of Hastings, Gytha tried to buy his body from King William, offering to pay the weight of the body in gold. When her attempt failed she retired to live on her estates in Devon and Somerset, which she had been allowed to keep after the Norman victory.

Gytha was not prepared to give in to the new king without a fight, as Source C shows.

In 1068, when William demanded the submission of Exeter, its citizens refused. Instead, they unwisely tried to bargain with the king. They would not let him into the city and would only pay traditional taxes they had always paid the king.
William blockaded the city walls, refusing to let anyone in or out. He took hostages from surrounding villages and demanded surrender. But still the people resisted. They sent William a message that said: 'We shall not swear an oath of fidelity to the pretended king, nor admit him within our walls.'
One rebel stood on the castle wall, bared his bottom and broke wind in front of the Normans! William was furious. He took hostages in front of the city walls and ordered his soldiers to put out the eyes of one of them. But this only made the English people more determined to resist.
After eighteen days, William managed to gain entry to the city and Exeter was forced to surrender. One account claims that the king was able to enter because parts of the city wall had fallen down. But another account states that the citizens had to surrender because their own nobles had betrayed them.
Gytha and her companions escaped from the city before its surrender, taking with them a great store of treasure. At first Gytha stayed on an island in the Severn Estuary. But eventually, she settled in Denmark. The resistance of the Godwin family was over.

**A modern account of Gytha's rebellion, based on eyewitness stories.**

# TASKS...

1. **a)** The map on page 51 suggests that, by 1066, William was in control of the eastern Fens. Do you think this is true?

   **b)** Do you agree with the map when it suggests that, by 1070, William was in control of almost all of England? Give reasons for your answer.

2. Look at Source A. Do you think the artist admired Hereward or not? Use details from the source to support your answer.

3. Does Source A give us a reliable picture of Hereward? Explain your answer.

4. Read Source B. Do you think this story could be true? Give reasons for your answer.

5. Read Source C.

   **a)** *Either* write a newspaper account of Gytha's rebellion in Exeter from an English point of view.

   **b)** *Or* write entries in Gytha's diary during the siege of Exeter. **WS**

## Plenary

Why do you think it was so important for English people to have stories like those in Sources B and C in the years after William's invasion?

# HOW DID WILLIAM TAKE CONTROL OF THE REST OF THE COUNTRY?

By the end of this section you will be able to answer these questions.
- How much resistance to the Normans was offered by the English people?
- How quickly did William of Normandy gain control of England?

You will analyse sources to answer these questions.

## Starter

*Imagine you are William's number one adviser. It is 1070 and William is keen to return to Normandy to spend some time with his friends and family. He wants to know whether he can safely leave England in the hands of his loyal supporters without the English overthrowing him when he has gone. Write a paragraph to William giving your opinion on whether it is safe for him to leave at this time. Think about everything that has happened between 1066 and now before you write your advice. Be prepared to share this advice with others in the class.*

## Opposition to William

Hereward's rebellion was one of many that William had to deal with in the years after the Battle of Hastings. This victory was just the beginning of a campaign that would last for several years – a campaign in which William fought to gain control over England. Historians do not agree on how quickly William managed to get this control. Read Source A and pick out three methods William used to gain control. You could make this a spider diagram or a mind map.

## How quickly did William gain control?

Look at Sources B and C. As you will see, historians have different views about how quickly William managed to take a firm hold of England. What these historians think is important, but these sources may also help you to answer the bigger question: *'Did William's conquest change England?'*. Do you think that William's invasion changed life dramatically for the English people? If so, you might expect that William established his control quickly. Think carefully about your own views as you read the sources.

**SOURCE A**

1066 · Dover surrenders to the Normans without a fight.
· William marches to London destroying property, stealing food and killing many English.
· Prince Edgar, Earl Edwin and Earl Morcar surrender.
· William is crowned King of England.
· Monks at Peterborough say that Edgar is the true king of England and elect a new **abbot**. William collects a fine after sending an army to threaten the monks.

1067 · William crushes a rebellion in Kent.

1068 · Rebellion in Exeter.
· Townsfolk refuse to surrender.
· Rebellion lasts for eighteen days.
· Rising in Durham leads to the massacre of the new Norman Earl of Northumberland and 900 followers.
· William kills hundreds and sets fire to Durham.
· Bristol and Gloucester are taken by William.

1069 · Rising in York led by Prince Edgar, supported by King of Denmark.
· William's castle in York is burnt down and Norman soldiers are killed.
· William bribes Danes to stay away from York, then retakes York by force.

· All crops, herds, flocks and food north of River Humber are burnt and destroyed.
· About 100,000 people die in the famine. (This becomes known as 'The Harrying of the North'.)

1070 · Rising in the Fens led by Hereward the Wake.
· It is eventually defeated one year later.
· Morcar is taken prisoner and Edwin is murdered.
· Hereward escapes.

1072 · Rising by the Scots led by Malcolm, King of Scots, supported by Prince Edgar.
· Scots surrender as soon as William sends in his armies.

1075 · Rising led by the Earls of East Anglia and Hereford. (This becomes known as 'The Revolt of the Earls').
· By rising at the same time in different places, they hope to split the Norman armies.
· William crushes rebels in Hereford before defeating rebels in East Anglia.

1080 · Norman bishop of Durham and 100 supporters are murdered by rebels in Northumberland.

1086 · Prince Edgar leads a revolt with help from the Danes.
· Rising comes to nothing.

1087 · Death of William.

**A list of events from various accounts written by twelfth-century monks.**

### Key words

**Abbot** A Church leader who supervises monks.

**SOURCE B**

By spring 1070, William was in control. Although there were other rebellions, none of them was as serious as the rebellions of 1067 and 1069.

**A modern historian writing in a textbook in 2000.**

DID WILLIAM'S CONQUEST CHANGE ENGLAND?

Many people (including several historians) think that the English stopped resisting the Normans after they had lost their king, most of the nobility and the best fighting men. Nothing could be more wrong. From the fierce fighting at the Battle of Hastings to the last rebellion twenty years later, the Normans had little peace from their English subjects.

**From an article on the Internet about 1066.**

## TASKS...

**1** Draw a table in your books like the one below.

| Date | William's actions | English resistance |
|------|-------------------|--------------------|
|      |                   |                    |

Complete the table by using details from the timeline on page 55.

**2** Working in pairs, decide whether the following statements are true or false, explaining how you reached your decision on each statement.

**a)** William only took harsh action against the English when they strongly resisted him.

**b)** William's actions against the English got more fierce as the years went by.

**c)** William was resisted by the English everywhere he went.

**d)** Most of the English resistance to William came after 1075.

**3** Why do you think it is so difficult to judge when William had control of the whole of England?

## EXTENSION TASK...

**4** Design a poster about 'The Harrying of the North' after the rising in York in 1069 to show the people of Britain the truth about William's cruelty. You should design your poster from an English point of view.

## Plenary

By which date do you think William was in control of England?

- 1070
- 1072
- 1075
- 1080
- 1087

Explain your answers. You may change your opinion as you work through the next sections!

# THE FEUDAL SYSTEM: A WORLD TURNED UPSIDE DOWN?

**Objectives**

By the end of this section you will be able to answer these questions.
- What was the feudal system?
- Was this system completely new after 1066?
- How did land ownership change after 1066?

You will use sources to compare life before and after 1066.

## Starter

*Look at Sources A and B. Both pictures come from manuscripts that show scenes from life in the Middle Ages. They show the king with some of his people.*

SOURCE (A)

**A twelfth-century painting of William with Alan of Brittany.**

SOURCE (B)

**A twelfth-century picture of a noble with the king.**

💡 *In each picture, who do you think is in control? How can you tell?*

💡 *Why do you think the knights are standing behind the king in Source A?*

💡 *In Source A, there is another person in the picture apart from the king and the knights. Who do you think this person is and what do you think he is doing?*

💡 *What do you think Sources A and B tell us about the relationship between the king and the people in the Middle Ages?*

## What was England like before 1066?

Look at the diagram below, which shows the way English people were organised before 1066.

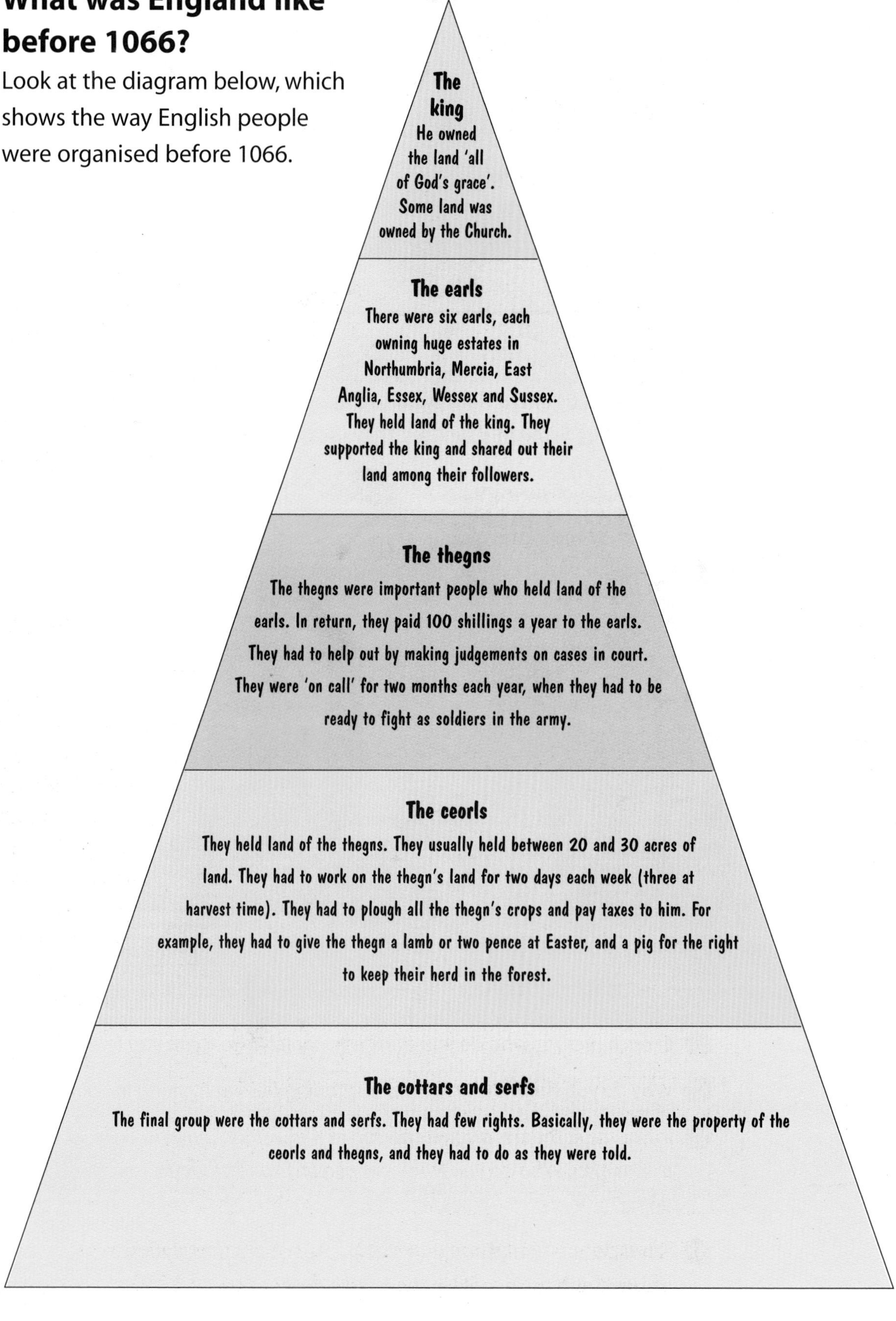

**The king**
He owned the land 'all of God's grace'. Some land was owned by the Church.

**The earls**
There were six earls, each owning huge estates in Northumbria, Mercia, East Anglia, Essex, Wessex and Sussex. They held land of the king. They supported the king and shared out their land among their followers.

**The thegns**
The thegns were important people who held land of the earls. In return, they paid 100 shillings a year to the earls. They had to help out by making judgements on cases in court. They were 'on call' for two months each year, when they had to be ready to fight as soldiers in the army.

**The ceorls**
They held land of the thegns. They usually held between 20 and 30 acres of land. They had to work on the thegn's land for two days each week (three at harvest time). They had to plough all the thegn's crops and pay taxes to him. For example, they had to give the thegn a lamb or two pence at Easter, and a pig for the right to keep their herd in the forest.

**The cottars and serfs**
The final group were the cottars and serfs. They had few rights. Basically, they were the property of the ceorls and thegns, and they had to do as they were told.

# The feudal system after 1066

### The king

William kept 20 per cent of the land in England for himself. He gave 25 per cent of the rest to the Church. What was left was shared between his followers. There were only about 180 of them.

### The barons

These followers were barons. They became known as tenants-in-chief. In return for their land they took oaths of loyalty to William and promised to give his army money or soldiers. They kept some land for themselves and split up the rest into manors, which they gave to their followers.

### The knights

These men were knights, who became known as under-tenants. In return for their land, they took an oath of loyalty to the baron and promised to serve as a knight in the army (fighting on horseback). They kept some land for themselves and shared the rest between the Saxon peasants, who lived on their manor.

### The villeins

These Saxons became known as villeins. In return for their land, they had to obey the lord of the manor and give him part of their crops. They also worked without pay on the lord's land. Villeins were not free men – they could not leave the lord's land without his permission. They even needed permission for their sons and daughters to get married!

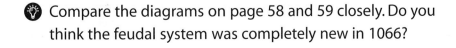 Compare the diagrams on page 58 and 59 closely. Do you think the feudal system was completely new in 1066?

## How the feudal system worked

'Feudum' is a Latin word meaning to give land in return for services. As king, William owned all the land in England. But he could not manage it on his own, and he wanted to reward those supporters who had helped him beat Harold in the Battle of Hastings. So he shared the land with his loyal followers.

William lent large estates of land to powerful barons. They gave smaller areas of this land, called manors, to knights. Knights were fighting men with little knowledge about farming. So they shared their manors among the peasants, or villeins, who worked on it.

Lending land in this way was called the feudal system. In the system, each person made promises in return for their land. The diagram on page 59 shows the promises that each person made so they could hold onto their land. It also shows how the different groups in society were arranged in a hierarchy.

💡 What do you think 'hierarchy' means? (You might have used this word when describing food chains in Science, or you might have used it in Geography.)

## How did the feudal system change England?

In 1086, William ordered a detailed survey to show who owned each piece of land, how much money the property was worth, and the numbers and types of people in each area. This was called the 'Domesday Survey'. It showed that only two of the great tenants-in-chief (barons) were English. The rest were Norman. The English earls and thegns had lost their wealth and power. It seemed like much had changed since 1066. But how big were these changes? Historians have different opinions about this, as you will see from sources C to F.

## SOURCE D

Knight service was new in the feudal system. Although military service was a duty performed by thegns before 1066, they were foot soldiers, not knights. Knights were important (and rich) soldiers who fought on horseback. Knight service can be traced back to the reign of William the Conqueror, but no further. This, and taking an oath of loyalty to the king, was what made the feudal system new.

**An historian writing in 1968.**

## SOURCE E

Much is made of the 'newness' of the feudal system that followed the conquest. Apparently, holding land in exchange for military service was new. But even before 1066, landholders had to do military service. Although everything seemed to have changed after 1066, in many ways it was just the same.

**Adapted from an article on the Internet.**

## SOURCE F

Ideas about land holding and services were similar in England and Normandy before 1066. The conquest didn't introduce new systems of farming or land management. People still wore the same kinds of clothing and lived in the same types of houses as they did before the Norman Conquest. The new Norman king and his lords were not interested in changing the ways ordinary people lived their lives.

**An historian writing in 2002.**

The feudal system was a simple way of organising society. There were four main levels or ranks in the hierarchy (see page 59), each with its own set of rights and duties. Today, society is much more complicated.

## TASKS...

1 Think of six to ten different people in today's society – for example, teacher, doctor, lawyer, factory worker. Place them in order, with the most important at the top and the least important at the bottom. Compare your list with those of others in the class.

# TASKS...

**2 a)** Copy a chart like the one below into your book, using details from pages 58–61. You will need this information to help prepare a group report.

|  | Before 1066 | After 1066 |
|---|---|---|
| Who owned the land? |  |  |
| Did military service exist? |  |  |
| Who did military service? |  |  |
| Did everyone have to pay homage? |  |  |
| What was life like for ordinary people? |  |  |

**b)** Get into groups to prepare your report, which should answer the following questions. The information you already have in your charts will help.
- How 'new' was the feudal system?
- How do you think the feudal system helped William to gain control of England?

## Plenary

What were the main differences between the way England was organised before 1066, and after?

# HOW FAR DID WILLIAM CHANGE THE ENGLISH CHURCH?

**Objectives**

By the end of this section you will be able to answer these questions.
• How important was the Church in the Middle Ages?
• What changes did William make to the English Church?
You will write a persuasive letter about these changes.

## Starter

*What do you know about religious buildings? How often do you visit a religious building? In groups, draw a mind map about 'places of worship'. Include details about the buildings themselves, the different types of places of worship, the people who work there, the different services that are held there, and whether a place of worship is important in your everyday life.*

## The importance of the Church

In the Middle Ages, the Church played a very important part in peoples' lives. Look at the diagram on page 64, which shows how the Church was organised and how it supported local people.

### Ordinary people and the Church

In the Middle Ages, people went to **church** regularly. Church services were in Latin, which most ordinary people couldn't understand. Most ordinary people couldn't read or write, either. Instead, they learned from listening to the priest's sermon or by looking at the wall paintings, which often showed grim pictures of what it was like in hell.

To avoid going to hell, people had to confess their sins to the local priest and show they were sorry for committing them. The priest also married people in church, baptised their babies and forgave the sins of people who were dying. These were all important stages in people's lives. So the priest was obviously one of the most important men in the village.

The **Church** had a huge influence on people's minds. It reminded them that if they were bad, they would go to hell when they died, but that if they were good, they would go to heaven. Any king who could control the Church could also control the people.

### Key words

**church** When a small 'c' is used, it means a local, or parish, church.

**Church** For this period when a capital 'C' is used, it refers to the whole of the Catholic Church led by the Pope.

💡 How do you think controlling the Church helped William to control the country?

**The Pope.**
• Head of the Catholic Church in all of Western Europe.
• All kings, princes and emperors obeyed him.

💡 If you were in William's position, how would you try to take control of the Church? You could brainstorm some ideas in pairs before you read on.

**Bishops, Archbishops and Cardinals.**
• Advised kings and emperors on how to govern their people.
• Became statesmen and diplomats.

**Parish priest.**
• Responsible for the parish church and his parishioners.
• Advised on spiritual matters.
• Taught the meaning of religion.
• Baptised, married and buried people.
• The parish church was a central place for community affairs, entertainment and socialising.

**Monks and nuns.**
• Worshipped privately in a monastery (monks) or a nunnery (nuns).
• Often conributed to the life of the community, caring for sick and poor people.
• Shut themselves away from the world in order to get closer to God.

**Friars.**
• Friars were travelling monks.
• They wandered from village to village, working and begging for food.
• They helped the sick in their homes, taught religious lessons, and carried news from village to village.

### How William used his own men to work in the Church

First, William appointed Lanfranc, an abbot from Normandy, as the Archbishop of Canterbury. This was the most important job in the English Church, so William wanted to make sure the archbishop was a loyal follower of his.

Then he granted large areas of land to bishops and abbots. He brought many new Church leaders to England from Normandy. He chose some of them as bishops because they were holy men. But he chose others because they were loyal soldiers to him. In 1066, there were sixteen bishops in total, and all of them were English. By 1080, fifteen of the sixteen bishops were Norman. The bishops replaced some of the local priests with Norman ones, but most were still English.

### Changing Church customs and practices

The new Norman Church leaders began to introduce their own ideas into church services. The abbot of Glastonbury made the monks sing Norman prayers. When they refused, he sent for some knights who broke down the abbey doors and killed three monks, wounding eighteen more. At Evesham, the relics of English saints were set on fire. At Ely, the finest church treasures were seized and placed in William's treasury.

The Church calendar listed all the important religious events and festivals during the year. It told people which were Saints' days, and advised them what to do on certain other days of the year. This calendar was changed by the bishops, and all apart from two of the English Saints' days were removed. The priests were given new strict rules. These rules said they could no longer get married. They should dress in simple clothes, have their hair cut and rounded so that their ears could be seen, and stay out of inns and taverns.

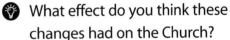 What effect do you think these changes had on the Church?

### Building new churches

William built new churches and cathedrals. English churches were usually quite small and made of wood. Norman churches were larger and made of stone. The map on this page shows the new cathedrals built by the Normans. The photograph on page 66 shows Winchester Cathedral which was begun in 1079.

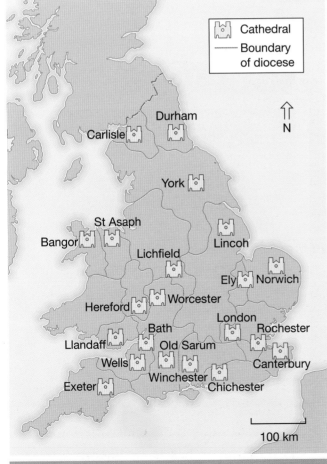

**Places where the Normans built new cathedrals.**

## SOURCE A

**An aerial view of Winchester Cathedral.**

💡 Using Sources B and C, list the differences you can spot between English and Norman churches.

Some English people might have been impressed with the strong stone Norman buildings, but not everyone agreed. In 1084, an English monk complained that holy men were too busy caring for church buildings and not spending enough time looking after people's souls.

## SOURCE B

**A small English church built in the ninth century in Essex. The church is made from wood.**

## SOURCE C

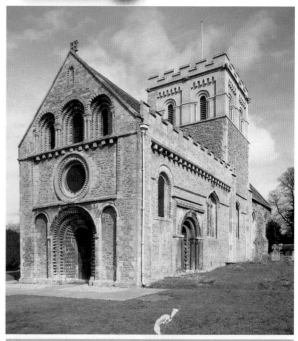

**A church rebuilt by the Normans in Iffley, (Oxford), in the twelfth century.**

# TASKS...

**1** Do you think William's changes improved the Church or not? Gather evidence from pages 63–6 and from your own reading to show:

   **a)** the ways in which the Church improved

   **b)** the ways in which the Church stayed the same or even got worse.

## EXTENSION TASK ...

**2** Imagine you are a priest in 1087. Write a letter to your local tenant-in-chief complaining about the changes William has made to the Church. Try to persuade the tenant-in-chief that now William is dead, it is time to change some things back again. The guidelines below will help you. **WS**

### The purpose of your letter

- To argue that William's changes have been bad for the Church.
- To make the tenant-in-chief think about asking the new king to bring back some of the old ways of the Church.
- To make the tenant-in-chief think that if he fails to act on your letter, he will be letting both God and himself down, and putting his family's future in heaven at risk.

### The text level

- Use different sizes of print and fonts to emphasise your points.
- Start with three or four powerful opening statements about how the Church has 'fallen into bad ways' during the reign of William. Back up each of these statements with evidence. End by repeating the arguments and concluding, that unless things go back to how they were before William's arrival in England, the future is very gloomy indeed.
- Use illustrations in your letter, either in the form of writing or pictures, to show the bad state of the English Church.

### The sentence level

- Write your letter in the first person.
- After your first three or four opening statements, use short sentences to emphasise all the evidence that shows things have gone wrong in the Church. Use examples from the church at which you are the priest.
- Use connectives that are related to logic – like *this shows*, *because*, *therefore* and *in fact*.
- Use opinions that are different to your own, so that you can disagree with them in your letter. For example:

People have said that William's changes have brought fresh energy to the Church at a time when it was in need of it. Nothing could be further from the truth. My church has always been well attended. All these new services and prayers in French that his Holiness the Bishop is insisting on are just confusing people and making it hard for them to reach God.

### The word level

- Use value judgement words to influence the tenant-in-chief such as *obviously, vital, scandal, criminal, the work of the devil*.
- Choose adjectives and adverbs for their emotional effect and impact on the tenant-in-chief.

# HOW DID CASTLES CHANGE THE ENGLISH LANDSCAPE?

**Objectives**

By the end of this section you will be able to answer these questions.
* What were the first Norman castles like?
* Where did William the Conqueror build castles?
* How did the castles affect the lives of English people between 1066 and 1087?

You will also be asked to:
* write a report
* use sources to analyse the effects of castles from an English viewpoint.

## Starter

*Have you ever seen a castle? What does a castle look like? From memory, draw a picture of a castle and label as many different parts of it as you can. Compare your castle with castles drawn by other classmates. How are they similar and how are they different?*

## William's network of castles

**Key words**

**Strategic** Carefully chosen. You often use this word if you are talking about military plans.

Look at Source A on page 69. It is a modern artist's impression of a typical Norman castle built shortly after 1066.

You have already learned from pages 54–67 that, after the invasion, William spent a long time trying to gain control of his new kingdom. One method he used was to build a network of castles (like the one in Source A) at key places known as 'strategic' points'. Page 71 tells you how many castles William built after 1066.

### Typical features of early Norman castles
* The castle builders first built up a mound of earth, called a motte.
* Around the bottom of this was a deep ditch.
* On top of the motte they built a wooden wall called a stockade, or a palisade.

## Key words

**Drawbridge** A bridge that can be raised or lowered to stop people getting in or out.

- Inside the stockade they added a wooden tower, or keep.
- Next to the motte was a yard with a stockade, ditch and bank all round it. This was called a bailey (which is where the soldiers lived).
- If the castle was attacked, the soldiers would retreat inside the keep, crossing from the bailey into the motte by the wooden **drawbridge**.

## SOURCE A

**A typical Norman castle built after 1066.**

# TASKS...

1. If you were building a castle, what kind of place do you think would make a strategic point?

2. In pairs, brainstorm how you would attack a motte and bailey castle. You can only use methods that were available in the eleventh century.

3. Write a secret report to a local rebel leader in 1066, explaining your ideas on how you think a castle could be taken from the Normans. **WS**

4. Now imagine you are a Norman who has intercepted (got your hands on) the secret report. Either make a bullet-point list of the changes you could make in response to the report, or draw a version of the castle showing all the new features you think the Normans might have added in the 50 years after 1066. Label all the new features clearly. **WS**

# How did castles affect life in England after 1066?

## TASKS ...

1   Working in groups, look at Sources B to E. If you had been living in England in the Norman period, would you think that castles were a good or bad idea?

2   Study the sources and information carefully.

   a)   In your books, write the heading 'Castles make life better for English people'. On another page, write the heading 'Castles make life worse for the English people'. Using details from the sources, make notes under each heading. **WS**

   b)   When your notes are finished, discuss whether you think castles were good or bad for English people. **WS**

SOURCE  B

The English had to get used to the castles and seeing troops of heavily armed Norman knights riding through their towns and villages. These men were their new lords, men who spoke a different language, men who had the power of life or death over them.

**An extract from a modern school textbook written in 2002.**

**English peasants who have been turned out of their houses by the Normans in Lincoln. They are forced to begin work on building a castle on the site where their houses once stood.**

SOURCE  C

Some English people may have been grateful for castles. The areas around them were peaceful and each castle provided work for the English. Sometimes, the baron who supervised the building of the castle would try to get skilled craftsmen and their families to live near it. Huts and houses would be built around the castle walls, attracting further settlers like traders and innkeepers. Soon, towns began to develop in these places.

**An historian writing in 1997.**

The Normans often pulled down houses to make way for new castles. In Gloucester, 16 houses were pulled down; in Cambridge, the number was 27; in Norwich, it was 113; and in Lincoln, 166. Families who lost their homes had to look after themselves. They were often made to work as slaves to build castles on the very places their homes had stood.

**An extract from a book written in 1985.**

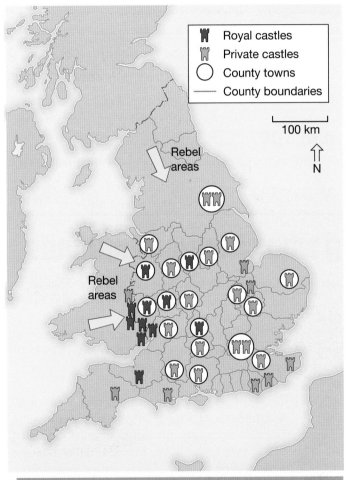

Royal castles
Private castles
County towns
County boundaries

100 km

N

Rebel areas

Rebel areas

**The royal and private castles built by William the Conqueror.**

It is not true that the English had no castles in 1066. Some Normans had already settled in England before 1066 and had built castles in Herefordshire, Essex and Dover. After 1066, new castles were built on older defensive sites. Lincoln castle was built on the site of a Roman fort and the Normans left the Roman walls standing. The Norman castle owners changed to English ways. The armies that were stationed in the castles were often made up of Norman and English soldiers. English people were often given important jobs in the castle, like collecting taxes from local people and working in the law courts. Eventually, English people married into Norman families.

**From a textbook about the Normans written in 2002.**

## Plenary

Imagine it is 1087 and news has just reached England that William has died. Using what you have learned so far in this chapter, write a paragraph to say how you feel about William's death. You can be either English or Norman.

DID WILLIAM'S CONQUEST CHANGE ENGLAND?

# HOW DID WILLIAM'S CONQUEST CHANGE ENGLAND?

**Objectives**

By the end of this section you will be able to answer these questions.
- Was the England of 1087 totally different from the England of 1066?
- Did English people benefit or suffer from the changes made by William?
- What was William's record as King of England like?

You will set out your conclusions in a structured essay.

## Starter

*Look back at the story told by the trader in the tavern at the beginning of this chapter (see pages 48–9). In his story, he describes his fears for England now that William is king. Was he right to be afraid? Remember your paragraph that you wrote for Task 2 on page 49. Now that you have studied this whole chapter, do you still agree with what you wrote?*

## William's reputation in 1087

Read the newspaper story below, then answer the questions that follow it.

---

*The Daily Norman*                                                                                    1087

# Shock death of king who changed England!

News has reached us from France that William is dead. He died in a tragic accident. He had just defeated rebels in France when his horse reared up. As he was thrown off the horse, he was fatally injured in the stomach by the front part of his saddle.

William had many achievements. By 1070, he had got England under control and had crushed all of the resistance to him, just four years after being crowned King of England. He built impressive new castles everywhere in England, which totally changed the landscape and people's lives. He replaced all the wooden churches with new stone ones, and he replaced all the old bishops and priests too, bringing new life to the Church.

William introduced the feudal system, which was completely new. This helped him to set up control and totally change the system of landholding.

Looking back over his reign as a whole, it is incredible to see what a difference he made. England today is totally different to the England that existed before 1066. May his soul rest in peace. Amen.

---

### Key words

**Biased** This is when someone has a point of view that is influenced by personal feelings or a lack of information.

- Which words and phrases do you think show whose side the writer is on?

- Is the writer **biased**?

- Who do you think might have written the story and why?

# TASKS...

1  In 1087, was England totally different to the England before 1066? Write an essay about whether William's conquest changed England. Think about the following questions.

- What did the English think about their new king in 1066?
- How soon did William defeat his English opponents?
- Did castles change the landscape everywhere in England?
- Was the feudal system totally new?

- How far did William change the Church?
- How did William's conquest affect different people – for example, earls and thegns, cottars and serfs, bishops and priests? Would they all have had the same opinion about William's reign?

Give your conclusion to the key question: *'Did William's conquest change England?'*

Use the following guide to help you write your essay.

- Choose an appropriate title.
- Write an introduction that sets out the issue and states your aims.
- Put each new point in a separate paragraph. Start each paragraph with a topic sentence that introduces the point you are going to make clearly and directly.
- Support the argument in each paragraph by adding detailed evidence from your reading.
- Use quotes from your reading to support your arguments.
- Write in the third person and past tense when you are describing events and changes, and in the first person and the present tense when you are giving your personal views.
- Use connectives. For example:
  - when putting events into sequence, use next, then, first, second, third, finally, meanwhile, after
  - when comparing and contrasting, use equally, in the same way, similarly, likewise, whereas, instead of, alternatively, otherwise
  - when explaining the cause and effect of events, use because, so, therefore, thus, consequently
  - when supporting your views with evidence, use for example, such as, for instance, as shown by, in the case of.
- Write a summary and conclusion that sets out your overall opinion about the question you were set.

In your essay, make sure that:

- you have covered all the issues raised in the chapter
- each paragraph contains a separate point, introduced clearly and supported with evidence
- you have selected and organised the information well
- you have used appropriate connectives
- you have reached a fair and balanced conclusion.

## EXTENSION TASK...

2 Create your own newspaper story about the events of William's reign, written from an English point of view.

  a) Think about the type of newspaper you are writing for. Is it going to be a tabloid paper like the *Daily Mirror*, or will it be a broadsheet, like *The Times*? This will affect your writing style.

  b) Choose a gripping headline, and use persuasive language and short, punchy sentences.

  c) Think carefully about your choice of pictures to go with the piece. What purpose do you want them to serve?

## Plenary

You have learned a lot of new words in this chapter. You could play a word game like 'Word bingo' or 'Odd One Out' to test how much you have learned. **WS**

# WAS MEDIEVAL MEDICINE ALL 'DOOM AND GLOOM'?

## 3

## TIMELINE
### The development of medicine, 1066–1500

**1066** No one understood that germs caused diseases, so cleanliness was not considered to be important.

**1096** The Crusades to the Holy Land began. People returning from these Crusades brought back new ideas about medicine from Arab doctors.

**1237** Pipes were laid to carry clean water from the countryside into London. Most townspeople at this time got their water from polluted rivers.

**1272** A priest named Roger Bacon was put into prison for suggesting that doctors should experiment with their own ideas rather than rely on old methods.

**1349** The Black Death (plague) spread across Europe. Estimates suggest that one in three people died.

**1400** The Christian Church ended its ban on the dissection of human bodies around this time.

**1448** The development of the first printing presses meant that ideas about medicine could circulate more widely.

In this chapter you will:

- Explore medieval attitudes to medicine, health and hygiene.

- Find out what medieval people thought about the causes of, and cures for, disease.

- Discover their approach to childbirth and the raising of children.

- Investigate the state of hygiene in medieval towns.

- Work in lots of different ways, using diagrams and pictures as well as writing.

- Produce a piece of extended writing, using all the evidence you have looked at, to answer the question, 'Was medieval medicine all gloom and doom?'

*Look at the illustration below. The picture is of a scene in the Middle Ages.*

**Parents mourn a young victim of the Black Death. Estimates suggest that one in three people died from this plague.**

💡 *Use the 5Ws strategy (who, when, where, what and why?) to find out as much as you can from this picture.*

💡 *Share your questions with the class. Choose some of the best ones to display and see if the class can answer them over the next few lessons.*

# WHAT WERE HOSPITALS LIKE AND HOW WERE THE SICK TREATED IN THEM?

**Objectives**

By the end of this section you will be able to:
- compare a scene in a modern hospital with a scene showing treatment in the Middle Ages
- investigate how much sources can tell us about medieval medicine.

## Starter

*Have you ever been in a hospital? What was it like?*

*In groups, carry out a brainstorming activity about what it might be like inside a modern hospital. Write down all the words and phrases that your group can think of. Try to arrange your ideas under relevant headings. You could draw lines to connect ideas.*

## Treatment of the sick

Modern hospitals might be scary places, but they are very different to the places where medical treatment was carried out in the Middle Ages.

### Key words

**Lepers** People who suffer from a disease called leprosy. The disease makes skin rot, causing deformities.

**Maternity** Motherhood.

**Mute** Unable to speak.

From the 1100s onwards, the Church began to teach that it was a person's duty to care for the sick and it began to build hospitals, which were run by monks and nuns. Historians believe that there were probably about 1200 hospitals in England and Wales in the Middle Ages. However, only about 10 per cent of these hospitals actually cared for the sick. Some hospitals simply gave travellers and pilgrims somewhere to shelter, and about a third of hospitals were set up to house **lepers** – that is, to keep lepers away from the rest of society, not to treat their illness! Almost half of all medieval hospitals were simply places of rest or 'hospitality' for the poor and elderly. Such places did not provide medical care.

Some of the medieval hospitals were quite large, with spaces for over 200 patients. Four hospitals specialised in **maternity** cases, and there was one hospital for the blind, deaf and **mute**. Source A on page 78 shows Christian nuns in a fifteenth century hospital.

What can you learn from Source A about the similarities and differences between medieval and modern hospitals?

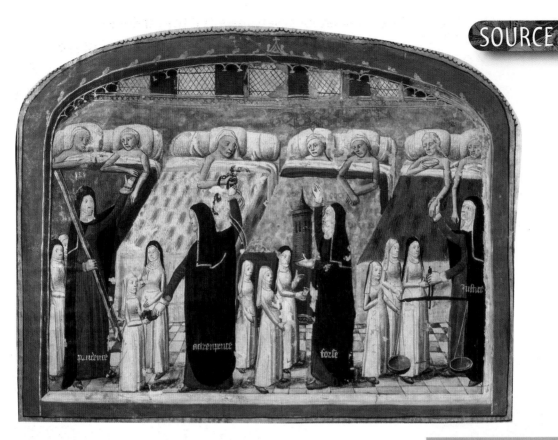

Christian nuns in a fifteenth-century hospital.

### *Painful operations*

Because no one knew about germs and the importance of cleanliness in the Middle Ages, many patients died even after small operations. This meant that operations tended to be done for only the simplest things or as a last resort when everything else had failed. Fractured bones, dislocated joints or injuries from war wounds often led to **amputations**. Death might quickly result after an amputation, either through loss of blood or the shock caused by the pain of the operation. Sometimes patients were given a mixture of opium and herbs to deaden the pain, but they would still have experienced great agony during the operation.

### Key words

**Amputation** When you have one of your limbs removed.

### *Barber-surgeons*

For most ordinary people, operations were carried out in shops owned by 'barber-surgeons'. These were people who were able to cut hair and pull teeth.

**Blood letting** When you cut the skin to make it bleed. People used to think you could cure an illness by getting rid of 'excess' blood.

They trained for seven years, but their training concentrated on things like the importance of **blood letting** and on superstitions – for example, which days of the year were 'unlucky' operating days. Barber-surgeons did not wear any special clothing and their instruments were not clean. On the days when they performed operations, they hung their blood-stained towels outside on a white pole. (You may have noticed that some modern-day barber shops still have a red and white pole outside.)

Barber-surgeons had no formal qualifications. So they were generally looked down on by other people in the medieval medical profession. However, they were popular because they offered many people their only hope of treatment.

## SOURCE B

The pole outside a modern-day barber shop.

## SOURCE C

An engraving from 1556 by Pieter Bruegel. His aim here was to make fun of the work of barber-surgeons.

# TASKS...

1   Study the information about the way sick people were treated in the Middle Ages and Sources A and C. Produce a mind map to show:
*The differences between medieval and modern hospitals and the treatment of the sick.*
Remember to use separate branches to organise your ideas.

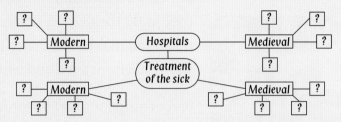

2   **a)**   In groups, study the sets of words in the box below. These words help to describe some of the key features of hospitals and treatment of the sick during the Middle Ages.
You should already be familiar with most of these words, but if there are any words that your group has not seen before, or if there are any words that you are unsure of, look up their meanings so that the whole group is in agreement about the definitions to be used for them.

**b)**   Take each of the words and place them under the headings 'Medieval' and 'Modern', depending on where your group thinks they belong. Some words may be difficult to place. If you cannot decide, place a copy of each of these words under both headings and be ready to explain why you have done this. **WS**

3   Now in your group, arrange the words again under two *different* headings: '*Helpful things about medieval hospitals and treatment*', and '*Harmful things about medieval hospitals and treatment*'. Repeat the procedures you followed in Task 2 above. **WS**

## Plenary

Think of one piece of advice you would give to a barber-surgeon to help improve his survival rates.

# HOW EFFECTIVE WERE MEDIEVAL DOCTORS?

**Objectives**

By the end of this section you will be able to answer these questions.
• What did medieval people think about the causes of disease?
• How did doctors diagnose and treat illness and disease?
You will extract information and organise it for a presentation.

## Starter

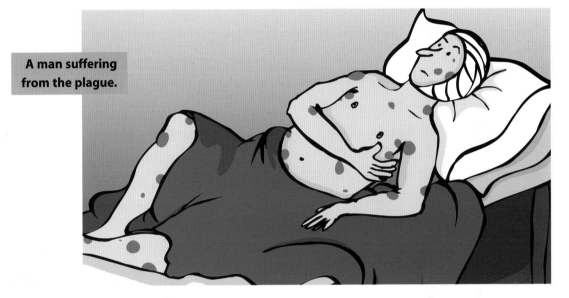

**A man suffering from the plague.**

### Key words

**Diagnosis** Identifying a disease based on its signs and symptons.

**Treatment** Care or attention from a doctor, to relieve illness or injury.

*If this person visited a doctor today, what do you think would happen? In pairs, make a list of the things you would expect the doctor to do. Divide your list into two columns headed* **'Diagnosis'** *and* **'Treatment'.**

## TASKS...

**1** In this activity, you will investigate the work of medieval doctors.
  • Your aim is to produce an illustrated talk about the work of medieval doctors.
  • Your talk should consist of a number of slides or information cards, which contain notes in bullet point form plus pictures and illustrations.
  • You could produce these on card, overhead projector transparencies or using a presentation package such as PowerPoint.
  • You will need to decide how to share out the work in your group and how to ensure that everyone is working towards the same end product. **WS**

# TASKS...

You can use the information on the following pages, but you must summarise the information, picking out key points rather than copying material out! Try to use other resources to find extra information.

As preparation, get a large sheet of paper and divide it into four columns as follows.

| Causes of disease | Methods of diagnosis | Treatment of everyday illnesses | Development of knowledge and skills |
|---|---|---|---|
|  |  |  |  |

When you have finished this preparation work, you should be ready to start work on your slides.

## Causes of disease

Medieval doctors did not understand that germs caused disease. They had a mixture of common-sense ideas and ideas based on superstitions to help them reach their own understanding about why diseases happened. In Sources A to D you should be able to find four different views about the causes of disease.

God is terrible towards the sons of men … He often allows plagues, miserable famines, conflicts, wars and other forms of suffering to arise, and uses them to terrify and torment people and so drive out their sins. And so the people of England are to be oppressed by the plague.

**From a monk's letter to the Bishop of London, 1348.**

The general cause [of the plague] was the close position of the three great planets, Saturn, Jupiter and Mars. This had taken place in 1345 on 24 March. Such a coming together of planets is always a sign of wonderful, terrible or violent things to come.

**Guy de Chauliac, a famous doctor writing in the 1300s.**

Medieval doctors thought that the body was made up of four humours – earth, fire, water and air. If these humours should get out of balance, you fell ill. In summer, the dry heat would increase the fire so you would sweat and get very hot – you might even become bad tempered. In winter, the damp climate would increase the water in your body. This would make you produce more phlegm and suffer from coughs and colds.

**From a textbook published in 1991.**

In the Middle Ages, people thought that worms were connected to illness … When doctors examined the faeces of sick people they often saw worms. It seemed obvious to link these to whatever illness the person was suffering from.

**From a textbook published in 1996.**

Which of the ideas in Sources A to D were based on common sense? Which were based on superstition?

## Methods of diagnosis

People believed that doctors should know how to write and speak well and have a good mind, so they trained for many years and studied from books written in Greek and Latin. They needed to study arithmetic, so they could count the number of hours a patient had been in pain. It was also believed that doctors should have a good knowledge of music, which people thought was a great help to the sick. People also thought that it was important to know about **astronomy** in order to understand the causes of disease.

Doctors sometimes checked the pulse of a patient and often studied the patient's urine. A chart told doctors what to look for in the urine. Clear urine indicated that the patient's digestion was good. Black and cloudy urine suggested that it was bad, and was taken as a sign of likely death. Diagnosing a patient's illness was done very differently to the methods used by doctors today, as Source E shows.

## SOURCE E

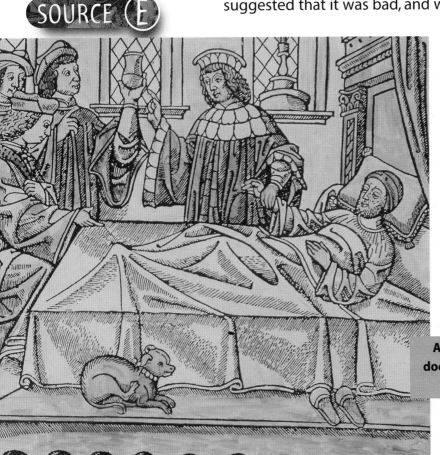

An engraving of a doctor examining a patient in 1345.

💡 What can you learn about medieval medical examinations from Source E?

# The treatment of everyday illnesses

Most illnesses were treated with herbal potions and mixtures. Doctors built up a great deal of knowledge about using herbs to treat everyday illnesses. Medical historians have studied the herbal mixtures used by medieval doctors and believe that a number of them probably worked well. However, some herbal treatments also relied heavily on superstition and 'magic', and were probably less successful. Some treatments were based on the theory of the four humours (see Source C on page 82). Medicines to get rid of blockages or 'excess blood' could sometimes be quite dangerous.

| ILLNESS | TREATMENT | |
|---------|-----------|---|
| Toothache | Take a candle of mutton fat, and burn it as close as possible to the tooth. Hold a basin of cold water beneath it. The worms that are gnawing the tooth will fall into the water to escape the heat of the candle. | Toothache |
| Heart disease | Give the patient a medicine of parsley or sage. Treat the patient with powdered animal skull, the juice of a boiled toad and dead insects. | Heart disease |
| Bad digestion | Remove the excess blood by cutting a vein. Alternatively use blood-sucking leeches. | |
| Eye infection | Make an eye-salve. To prepare the salve, take onion and garlic, equal amounts of both. Pound well together. Take wine and bull's gall, equal amounts of both. Mix with the onion and garlic, then put in a brass vessel. Let it stand for nine nights. Strain through a cloth and clear well. Put on the soreness with a feather. | Eye infection |
| Backache | Mix two pennyweights of betony (a herb) and two bowlfuls of sweet wine mixed with hot water. Give to a patient while fasting. | |
| Asthma | Put the lung of a fox into sweetened wine. Drink the mixture. | Backache |
| Sore eyelid | Poke the sore with nine grains of barley and say: 'Flee, flee, barley chase you.' | |

# Development of knowledge and skills

### Knowledge of anatomy

By the end of the Middle Ages, the skills of some doctors were improving with training in medical schools. In the fourteenth century, Guy de Chauliac, a French doctor, encouraged the **dissection** of dead bodies. Dissection was forbidden by the Church. However, De Chauliac claimed that by dissecting human bodies he had been able to learn the **anatomy** of internal organs, muscles, skin, veins and **sinews**. Gradually, medical schools allowed dissection to take place occasionally, as Source F shows. For example, at Montpellier in France after 1340, students were allowed to study one corpse a year – although the dissection was performed by the teacher's assistant, not the students.

> 💡 Why do you think the Church was against the dissection of corpses?

> 💡 How helpful do you think the study of corpses was to medical students in the Middle Ages?

### Use of anaesthetics

By the late-Middle Ages, more and more doctors were using simple **anaesthetics**. One recipe for an anaesthetic is given in Source G (see page 86). This mixture may have worked. It would certainly have sent patients to sleep, although great care would have been needed because if the dose was too strong it could have killed the patient! However, doctors were still only experimenting with anaesthetics at this time. More knowledge about the exact mixtures and doses of the different herbs and ingredients was needed.

(see page 86)

## Key words

**Dissection** When you cut open a body or object to examine its insides.

**Anatomy** The structure of a body.

**Sinews** Tough, elastic fibres that connect parts of the body together.

**Anaesthetics** Drugs given to a patient so no pain is felt during surgery.

## SOURCE F

**Medieval illustration of a teacher supervising a dissection at medical school.**

Take the **gall** of a boar, **hemlock** juice, lettuce, juice extracted from poppies, **henbane**, vinegar and wine. Let him that shall be carved sit against a good fire and make him drink until he falls asleep. Then you may safely carve him.

**A medieval recipe for anaesthetic.**

### Key words

**Gall** Digestive juices (bile).

**Hemlock** and **henbane** Poisonous herbs used in medicine.

### *The skills of surgeons*

When countries went to war in the Middle Ages, army surgeons travelled with regular soldiers. Many wounds needed to be treated on the battlefield, and the survival of wounded soldiers was important to the success of the army. Some army surgeons therefore began to experiment with treatments to try to reduce the number of deaths from war wounds.

John of Arderne served abroad as an army surgeon in the 1300s. He later worked as a surgeon in London and became one of the most famous surgeons in England. He developed new techniques for operations that were very successful. Some of them are still used today.

Wars encouraged people to experiment in other areas of surgery, too. New instruments and tools were developed. Theoderic of Lucca was a thirteenth-century surgeon. He believed that wounds would heal better if they were treated with wine to remove the pus from them. However, most ordinary people still relied on the barber-surgeons or their own 'tried and trusted' methods.

## Plenary

Prepare to feedback some or all of your presentation to the class.

# DID PEOPLE IN THE MIDDLE AGES CARE FOR THEIR CHILDREN?

**Objectives**

By the end of this section you will be able to answer these questions.
• What problems were associated with childbirth in the Middle Ages?
• How were children raised in the Middle Ages?

You will be able to weigh up evidence to reach a conclusion about whether medieval people cared for their children.

## Starter

*Look at the illustration above. It shows the birth of a baby in the Middle Ages. What are the chances of the birth being successful?*

💡 *Working with a partner, identify and explain all the things that would harm this woman's chances of giving birth successfully.*

*Now compare your work with the person beside you. Make a complete set of your answers.*

💡 *List all the things we do today to try to ensure that pregnant women give birth to healthy babies. Arrange these ideas under headings to describe what steps we take to ensure successful pregnancies.*

## Childbirth in the Middle Ages

In the Middle Ages, attitudes towards childbirth and methods of delivering babies were very different than they are today. Mothers would give birth to as many children as possible, because not all of them would survive. There were several reasons for such a high rate of infant mortality (death):

- There were no clinics in the Middle Ages, and no one was able to study babies in the womb using scanners and computers. There were no ways to tell whether a baby had a disease before it was born, as there are today.

- There was no advice from doctors and nurses on what or how the mother should eat, drink or behave during pregnancy. Many women carried on working hard up to the moment the child was born.

- Most babies were born at home, without injections or painkillers to help the mother to get through the pain of childbirth. Midwives were usually local women who had little medical training, at least not until the later Middle Ages.

- Midwives were able to carry out **caesarian section** operations to deliver babies that might not survive. These operations were carried out on kitchen tables and beds, not in hospital. Midwives often had unclean hands and wore their normal work clothes.

- There were no **incubators** to keep premature babies alive.

Giving birth was therefore a dangerous business in the Middle Ages. One in five pregnant women died either during childbirth or soon after. And even after a successful birth, a child's chances of survival were not good. Over half of all babies died before they reached their first birthday. A large number died before becoming an adult, and 40 was considered old age!

## How were children raised in the Middle Ages?

Most ordinary women led difficult lives in the Middle Ages. As well as taking care of their children they were expected to sweep the house, cook meals, brew ale, look after domestic animals, and tend the garden and the orchards. Children, even babies, had to fit into this lifestyle.

Women therefore swaddled their children. This meant wrapping them from head to toe in bandages so that they could not move, which allowed mothers to work while carrying their child. It was also convenient since it meant babies could be left unattended while the mother was at work; some mothers hung their babies on hooks to keep them out of harm's way. People also believed that swaddling a child would straighten out his or her limbs.

## How did children die?

Evidence given at coroners' inquests (see pages 90–1) into accidental deaths in Bedfordshire during the fourteenth century reveals that tragic deaths happened quite often.

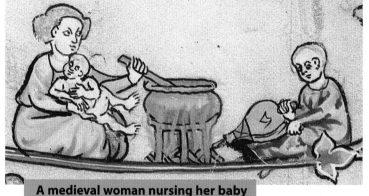

**A medieval woman nursing her baby while cooking at the same time.**

- *33 per cent of children under one year died in fires while in their cradles.*

- *21 per cent of unattended babies who were not in their cradles also died in house fires.*

- *46 per cent of babies who were more than one year old died while playing with water, pots, fire and other children.*

- *Older children often died as they tried to copy their mother or father. For example, a two-year-old girl tried to stir a pot of hot water, but tipped it onto herself and was scalded to death. A three year-old boy was following his father to the mill and drowned. Another was watching his father cut wood when the blade of the axe flew off the handle and struck him.*

## TASKS...

1 look at the percentage of babies dying due to fires in their cradles, house fires and playing with water, pots, fire and other children. Present this information in a different way. For example, you could produce a bar graph, a pictogram, or a pie chart.

### How did people react to the death of a child?

We might think that children were unloved in the Middle Ages, but this is not necessarily true. Families could be punished if their babies died by rolling into fires when left unattended. Priests in church sermons often pleaded with parents to take greater care, and asked

mothers to tie their cots safely so their babies could not fall out. Laws were passed which made sure that, when infants died in suspicious circumstances, the parents would be questioned to see if they had failed to care properly for their children.

💡 How responsible were parents for the accidental deaths of young children in the Middle Ages?

A medieval engraving showing the figure of Death (the skeleton) taking a young child from a poor house.

### Coroners

Some people did take the death of a child seriously in the Middle Ages. Any mysterious death had to be investigated by a coroner. The coroner would arrive with a clerk, who would record the statements of the family and neighbours about how the child died. This would include details of the activity that led to the death, the names of the first finder and other witnesses, the hour, date and location, and the child's age. These statements were then translated into Latin by the clerk. Next, the coroner had to inspect the body by stripping it and exploring the wounds. He had to try to find out the probable cause of death.

Statements made by family members and neighbours were always carefully checked by calling in four men from the surrounding area to act as character witnesses. They had to say whether the family was honest and of good standing.

If the coroner thought the child had been murdered, he had to decide who should be charged with the crime. If the death was accidental, he had to say what the cause of death was. He would then collect taxes from the family. These were paid so that prayers could be said for the soul of the dead child.

### Did parents love their children?

We can also find evidence about child deaths from stories told by travellers as they went on pilgrimages. A number of these stories were collected together in the fifteenth century. Many stories, such as the one in Source C, tell of the sadness of families who lost children in accidental deaths.

A girl of three years old was sitting under a large stack of firewood with other children who were playing by themselves, when a huge trunk fell and threw her on her back in the mud, pinning her down so heavily that she died. The horror of the sight soon scattered her friends, who ran to and fro in all directions. The child's father came up to see what had happened. His heart filled with grief. Lifting the log with some difficulty, he raised her in his hands. Then he cried and with heavy groans and loud wailing, he made for the church that stood near by.

**An extract from a collection of fifteenth-century stories.**

💡 If families were so upset by the deaths of their children, why didn't they do more to protect them?

According to historians, medieval people did not see it as their first duty to shower their children with affection and love. Life was harsh, so parents tried to raise their children to survive. The government did not take care of children as it does today. The survival of children depended on the child itself, and it was up to parents to make sure that their children could fend for themselves and learn how to survive. This might seem harsh to us today, but these were the popular ideas about raising children in the Middle Ages.

# TASKS...

**1** Gather evidence from your reading about whether medieval people cared for their children. Now read the following statement:

*'Medieval parents were cruel. They did not properly care for, or look after, their children.'*

**a)** Do you agree or disagree with this statement?

**b)** Draw a table with two columns like the one below and complete it using the evidence from pages 87–91.

| Parents did care for their children | Parents did not care for their children |
| --- | --- |
| | |

**c)** What is your overall conclusion? Share your findings with a partner and listen to what he or she has to say.

# EXTENSION TASK...

**2** Look again at the information about the death of a child in Source C on page 91. Imagine you are the coroner who has to carry out the inquest into the death and write a final report. Using the information about coroners on pages 90–1, write up the coroner's report using the following guide. **WS**

- The report should include a description of the evidence of the family and neighbours about how they discovered the dead child. It will also need a summary of the examination of the body, with a verdict about the cause of death, and an assessment of the amount of tax to be collected for the prayers for the soul of the dead child.

- The report should include questions to the family about how the body was discovered, and what the family and the child were doing at the time of the death. It will need to record the age of the child, the location of the death, and the names of the witnesses.

- You should also include the evidence of four character witnesses who will state how long they have known the family, what their relationships with the family are, and whether they can state that the family is honest and 'of good standing'.

- Make sure that your report 'fits' the details of the death described in Source C.

## Plenary

From all the work you have done in this section, pick out one piece of evidence that best shows, in your opinion, that parents did, or did not, care for their children. Explain why you have chosen that piece of evidence.

# HOW HEALTHY AND HYGIENIC WERE TOWNS IN THE MIDDLE AGES?

Objectives

By the end of this section you will be able to answer these questions.
- What was the state of health in a medieval town?
- Who was to blame for the state of the town?

During this lesson you will:
- take part in an investigation about the state of a medieval town.

## Starter

SOURCE (A)

SOURCE (B)

SOURCE (C)

*Sources A, B and C are signs that we encounter in modern life. They are example of signs about **hygiene**.*

 *In pairs, discuss the meaning of each sign. Are words or pictures being used, or both? Do you think the message of the sign will be clear to a passer-by, or to someone who does not understand English?*

*What would happen if you did not do what the sign said?*

*Do you think that signs about hygiene are important? Why do you think this?*

### Key words

**Hygiene** This is about making sure that living conditions are clean so that people stay healthy.

# Investigating Cessville – a medieval town

Study the illustration of an imaginary medieval town called Cessville below.

💡 What do you learn about living conditions in Cessville from the illustration?

💡 What do you think it would have been like to live in Cessville?

# TASKS...

You are going to investigate the state of health and hygiene in Cessville, an imaginary town which reflects medieval town life. Your task is to decide who is to blame for the poor living conditions in Cessville.

**1** Read the character information on pages 96–7.

   **a)** For each character, make a list of all the activities that could be unhygienic.

   **b)** How might these activities affect the people in Cessville?

# Who was to blame for the state of Cessville?

All of the following people live in the imaginary medieval town of Cessville.

**Mr Brown and Mr Green of Thomas Row** *live in one of the poorest parts of Cessville. The houses in their street are tightly packed together with no proper drains or sewers. They use a bucket for a toilet. Mr Brown usually tips his sewage (waste) into the river, but Mr Green usually piles up his sewage outside his house in the hope that it will either be washed away or taken away by someone else. Mr Brown and Mr Green are only doing what everyone else in the street does.*

**Mr Bullstrode** *is a local builder and makes most of his money from building houses. Cessville has a growing population and there is plenty of work for him. He has been instructed by the local council that all new houses must be built with a cesspit (where you can get rid of sewerage) below them lined with stone or brick, but these could be quite expensive to make. Mr Bullstrode doesn't want to talk about the incident last year when a man fell through a rotten floor and drowned in the cesspit of one of the houses he had built.*

**Mrs Atkins** *is a water seller. She likes to get fresh water from a local spring and can get a good price for it from rich people, who will pay Mrs Atkins more money than most ordinary people can earn in a week just to get fresh water. Ordinary people would like fresh water too but often they get their water from polluted rivers. Sometimes Mrs Atkins tells her poor customers that the water she sells them is fresh water, when in fact it comes directly from the river. The river water is usually polluted and contains many life-threatening germs.*

**Mrs Walters and her daughter, Mary,** *live on Cheapside. They can just about make ends meet. Mrs Walters makes sure that her children are dressed in clean clothes. She gets her daughter Mary to help her with the washing. They soak the clothes in the river, then beat them with a heavy wooden bat to loosen the dirt. They use plant sap to try to remove the worst stains. To make a lather, they use unripe conkers that have been chopped. Then they dip the clothes in the river water again to wash away the dirt.*

**Councillor Clifford** *lives in a mansion just outside Cessville and likes to visit only when he has to attend a council meeting. He does not believe it is the council's responsibility to keep the town clean. He believes the town is dirty because the people who live in it have made it that way. He is against paying people to become 'rakers' to keep the streets clean. He is also opposed to building public toilets on a bridge over the river. However, he does agree that the people who drop rubbish in the streets should be arrested.*

**Mr Bates** is a butcher and he has his own shop. He sells the best quality meat only, and his shop is fairly clean. He believes he provides an important service for the people of Cessville. He is ashamed to admit that he was arrested last year for throwing rotten blood and offal (internal organs like heart and kidneys) into the street. He claims that he had nowhere else to put it. He is worried about the state of Cessville. On the street where he lives, workmen have just finished laying a proper sewer to take away the waste. He wonders why these cannot be laid everywhere.

**Richard Cobb and Elizabeth Burns** are two of the town's newest rakers. They each work in a team which has its own horse, cart and rakes. Each team is given an area of the town to keep clean. Richard and Elizabeth take their work seriously. However, there never seems to be enough time to get their streets cleaned properly and to take away the rubbish. They have both appeared in court recently, accused of moving the rubbish from their own streets and dumping it in other streets that were patrolled by other rakers.

**Thomas Scott** is well known locally. He has no home of his own and depends on the charity shown by the other residents of Cessville. He has bad habits and a short temper. Last year he was fined by the court for punching two men. They had complained that they had seen him urinating in the street instead of using the common privy (toilet).

**Silas Smythe** is a local landholder. He owns a large amount of land in the fields that surround Cessville. He often makes the journey into town to collect sewage from outside peoples' homes. He pays good money to take the sewage away so that he can use it for manure on his fields to help his crops to grow. He would certainly be opposed to any attempts to stop people from piling sewage outside their homes.

## Plenary

Clearly more than one person is to blame for the state of Cessville. Place the characters in a rank order, showing who you think is most to blame at the top through to who is least to blame at the bottom. Be ready to explain and defend your choices.

# WAS MEDIEVAL MEDICINE ALL 'DOOM AND GLOOM'?

**Objectives**

By the end of this section you will be able to answer this question.
- What were the positive and negative aspects of medicine and health during the Middle Ages?

You will also produce a piece of extended writing about whether the state of medicine and health was better in 1500 than it was in 1066.

### Starter

*Look at Source A. Use the 5W's (who, when, where, what and why) to find out as much as you can from this picture. Share your questions with the class.*

**An illustration from a medieval manuscript showing an operation on a patient's head.**

*How would you feel if you had been operated on in this way?*

# Two views about medicine in the Middle Ages

Doctors are trained in universities but treatments, mostly involving the use of herbs, are based on the theory of the four humours. People worship in traditional ways so surgeons are looked down on. Much of the new learning in the medical schools doesn't affect the work of barber-surgeons, who use the same methods as they always have. They are very limited in what they do. People generally have better houses and a more varied diet these days. However, they don't tend to live to old age. No one knows exactly what causes diseases. Deadly infections, kill over 50 per cent of children before their first birthday.

Since the 1300s, the Church has set up universities where doctors can be trained. Armies take trained doctors to war with them where they gain experience as surgeons on the battlefields. Rulers have introduced measures to clean up towns. Merchants and scholars travel around Europe, spreading ideas about medicine and disease. New ideas are reaching Europe from doctors in the Middle East. The doctors of 1350 still read the books of the Ancient Greek doctor Galen, though some people are beginning to think for themselves. Gradually people are challenging old beliefs. New ideas are on the way!

# TASKS...

**1**  **a)**  Summarise the viewpoint of each speaker on page 99.

   **b)**  Which of the two views provides the more accurate description of medical development during the Middle Ages?

**2**  **a)**  Look back over this chapter as a whole. In pairs, make brief notes about the aspects of medical development. Arrange your notes in two columns: those that show there was little progress or development of ideas and methods during this time, and those that show there was development. You will need to make notes on:

- childbirth
- raising children
- ideas about the causes of disease
- methods of diagnosis

- treatment of everyday illnesses
- surgeons and operations
- hospitals
- health and hygiene in towns.

   **b)**  Are there more examples of things staying the same, or more examples of things getting better?

   **c)**  Did the things that got better affect most people in most places, or did they affect only a few people in a few places?

   **d)**  What is your view of the question: *'Was medieval medicine all doom and gloom?'*
   Discuss this in pairs, then join another pair of pupils and continue your discussion. How is their chart of notes similar to and different from yours? Can you explain any differences? Add any new notes that you think are relevant to your own chart.

# EXTENSION TASK...

**3**  Produce a piece of extended writing to answer the following question:
   *'Was medieval medicine all doom and gloom?*

   Use the following guide to help you write your essay.

- Write an introduction that sets out the issue and states your aims.
- Put each new point in a separate paragraph. Start each paragraph with a topic sentence that introduces the point you are going to make clearly and directly.
- Support the argument in each paragraph by adding detailed evidence from your reading.
- Use quotes from your reading to support your arguments.
- Write in the third person and past tense when you are describing events and changes, and in the first person and the present tense when you are giving your personal views.
- Use connectives. For example, when comparing and contrasting, use words like *equally, similarly, likewise, whereas, instead of*.
- When supporting your views with evidence, use words like: *for example, such as, for instance, as revealed by*.
- Write a summary and conclusion that sets out your overall opinion about the question.
- Look at the marking scheme, which your teacher will show you, to gain clues about how to be successful in your essay.

## Plenary

You have learned lots of new words in this chapter. You could play a word game, such as 'Odd One Out' or 'Word bingo', to test how much you have learned.

# WHAT WERE PEOPLE'S BELIEFS IN THE MIDDLE AGES?

## 4

## TIMELINE
### RELIGION IN THE MIDDLE AGES
#### – some important dates

**1066**     After the Norman Conquest, the Normans introduce new Church leaders to England. They set up many monasteries.

**c.1090**     In the late-eleventh century, many great cathedrals are built – for example, Durham Cathedral, which takes 37 years to finish.

**1154**     Henry II becomes king. He argues with the Church about who should punish priests.

**1170**     Thomas Becket is murdered in Canterbury Cathedral.

**1205**     King John argues with the Pope about who should be Archbishop of Canterbury.

This chapter looks at people's beliefs in the Middle Ages. It looks first at the main beliefs people had at the time. Then it describes life in a monastery, what pilgrimages were and why people went on Crusades. Finally, it considers the supernatural, before giving you the opportunity to bring together, in some tasks and activities, all you have learned in this chapter.

💡 *What do you think we believe in today? In groups, draw up a list of five things you all believe in. When you have finished, compare your list to the groups next to you. What do other people in your class believe in?*

The great cathedrals and churches built in the Middle Ages had a huge impact on ordinary people. Remember, buildings were much smaller than they are today, and there were no high-rise flats, car parks or shopping centres. In the Middle Ages, the only really impressive building in most towns and villages was the church.

💡 *What impression do you think the great cathedrals and churches would have had on medieval people?*

💡 *How might the size of medieval cathedrals and churches have influenced people's religious beliefs?*

# WHAT DID PEOPLE BELIEVE ABOUT RELIGION?

**Objectives**

By the end of this section you will be able to answer this question.
- What were the main beliefs of medieval people?

You will also use sources to gather evidence of what people believed in.

## Starter

*Discuss the things that you think medieval people would have believed in.
During your discussion, try to remember what you have already learned about
the Middle Ages. Write a list … you may want to refer to this later!*

## How sources help us to understand what medieval people believed in

In the Middle Ages the vast majority of people in England believed in God.
England was a Christian country and English people were members of the
Roman Catholic Church. As you read in Chapter 2 (pages 47–74), religion at
this time was very important. A small number of people in England were
Jews, roughly 5000 to 6000 out of a population in 1086 of about 1.5
million.

If you could travel back to the Middle Ages and interview someone about
his or her beliefs, the person would probably say the following things.

*I believe that if I commit lots of sins without asking God for forgiveness I will go to hell.*

*I believe that I must live my life according to the Ten Commandments in the Bible.*

*I believe that I must pray to the saints and go on pilgrimages.*

*I believe that I must respect the local priest.*

We know that this is what people believed in because of the evidence they left. Pictures and paintings were important in the Middle Ages for giving people information, because most people at the time could not read. Look closely at Sources A to D, which show pictures from the time.

A wall picture from a medieval church.

**Illustration from a fourteenth-century English manuscript. It shows an angel and a devil competing for the soul of a dead man.**

💡 Can you find the dead man's soul in Source B?

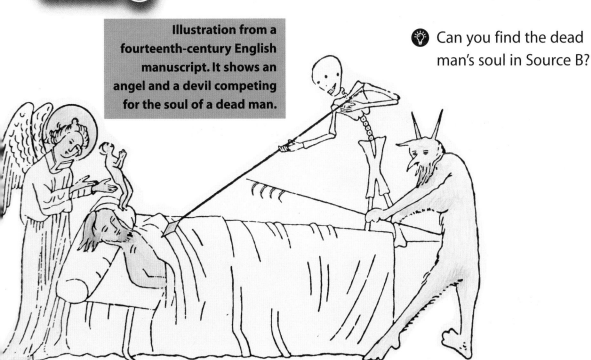

A fifteenth-century woodcut showing punishment for sins. Demons are torturing people by using a wheel to stretch their bodies.

## TASKS...

1 In pairs, use the 5Ws strategy to find out as much as you can about Sources A to D – *who, when, where, what and why*?

Write down down your findings.

SOURCE D

A medieval painting showing heaven and hell.

**2** What do Sources A to D tell us about people's beliefs in the Middle Ages?

When looking at Sources A to D you could ask the following questions:

- What was the person who drew or painted the picture trying to show?
- Was the person who drew or painted the picture trying to influence people?

Here are some words you might want to use to help you with your answers.

| hell | devil | angels | heaven | sinners |
|------|-------|--------|--------|---------|

You might also want to make a chart like the one below, which will help you to summarise your answers. An example has been done for you. **WS**

| | **What the picture actually shows** | **What the picture tells us about people's beliefs in the Middle Ages** |
|---|---|---|
| **Source A** | People being boiled alive or roasted over flames. | People must have believed that hell was a terrible place to go. |
| **Source B** | | |
| **Source C** | | |
| **Source D** | | |

**3** You will now give a report to the class about what Sources A to D reveal about people's beliefs in the Middle Ages. Remember to use evidence from the sources to back up your statements. **WS**

## Plenary

Look back at the list you made about the beliefs of medieval people at the beginning of this section. Do you still agree with this list? If your opinions have changed, how are they different?

# WHO KILLED NOVICE JOHN?

**Objectives**

By the end of this section you will find out:
- What was life like in a monastery?
- What was it like to be a monk or a nun?
- How important were the Church and religion in the Middle Ages?

You will also:
- understand that being an historian is a bit like being a detective
- analyse evidence to solve a murder investigation.

## Starter

*What do you think a monk or nun looks like? Have you ever seen a person who belongs to a religious community? What was the person wearing?*

*In pairs, discuss your answers. If it helps, you can draw pictures to describe your answers.*

## Monasteries, convents and the people who lived in them

In the Middle Ages, some people such as monks and nuns lived in religious communities called monasteries or convents. The rules in these religious communities were strict and the clothes worn by the monks or nuns were simple. They would wear long, rough woollen robes, called habits. The monks would shave the tops of their heads, so that they had a bald circle shape. A nun would wear a wimple, like a large hat that hid much of her face.

People who joined religious communities promised to live in poverty. This meant they had to give up everything they owned. They also made a promise of chastity, which meant they would no longer have sexual relationships. Finally, they promised the abbot or abbess (the head of the monasteries and convents) that they would be totally obedient and devote themselves to God. There were a number of religious orders that had different rules and practices. The largest order at the time was the Benedictines. Benedictine monks followed the Rule of St Benedict and were known as the Black Monks because of the colour of their habits. Other important religious orders included Cistercians, Carthusians and Augustinians.

Nuns at prayer.

Life was hard for the monks and nuns. They spent much of their day in prayer. They often had little to do with the outside world. When they weren't praying, they worked long hours in the fields, or cared for the sick or the dying.

Some monks illustrated, or illuminated, manuscripts, which was the way books were produced before the printing press was introduced. Look at Sources B, C and D, which show illustrated manuscripts.

The rules monks and nuns agreed to live by were strict, although they were not always obeyed.

💡 Why do you think people became monks and nuns?

## SOURCE B

This 'illuminated' manuscript is highly illustrated.

A medieval illustrated manuscript.

## SOURCE C

A medieval manuscript.

💡 How different are the manuscripts in Sources B, C and D to the books we read today? Try to come up with at least three points.

### *Bad behaviour!*

Not all monks and nuns followed a religious way of life marked by devotion, virtue and self-sacrifice. Reports by Church inspectors and in Church courts reveal that some monks and nuns were regularly breaking their religious vows during the Middle Ages. Reports describe cases of adultery, drinking and gambling, as well as laziness, greed and fighting. Some nuns were known to have had children!

However, although accounts of corruption in the Church would have made interesting gossip, most monks and nuns followed the rules of their religious order. They would have lived a life of prayer and discipline, helping the poor and sick and serving their local community, and would not have got into bad habits.

## A murder investigation

If there was a crime in a religious community, like a murder, the Church would investigate what happened. Imagine you are one of the Church's criminal investigators. You specialise in murder cases, and you have been asked by the abbott of Hestoneded Abbey to solve a crime. One of the abbey's novice (new) monks, called John, has been killed, and you must find the murderer. This investigation will involve a number of stages, and the information on pages 109–112 will help you.

**Who murdered the novice monk?**

# TASKS...

You are about to solve a murder. Here's how …

**Stage 1: gathering evidence**

When you get to the monastery, you ask the abbot for certain information to help you solve the crime. You need to know:

- the times of all the religious services.
- how many monks there are in the abbey, and who does which job.

The abbott gives you two pieces of evidence – Evidence A and Evidence B. Read these pieces of evidence carefully.

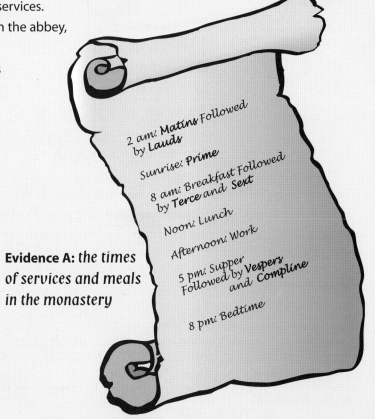

2 am: **Matins** Followed by **Lauds**

Sunrise: **Prime**

8 am: Breakfast Followed by **Terce** and **Sext**

Noon: Lunch

Afternoon: Work

5 pm: Supper Followed by **Vespers** and **Compline**

8 pm: Bedtime

**Evidence A:** *the times of services and meals in the monastery*

## Key words

**Matins** Morning prayer.
**Lauds** A short church service.
**Prime** A service held in the first hour of daylight.
**Terce** A service followed by reading and meditation.
**Sext** A service after which monks had a wash.
**Vespers** A service held in the early evening.
**Compline** The last service of the day.

**Evidence B:** *the monks and their jobs*

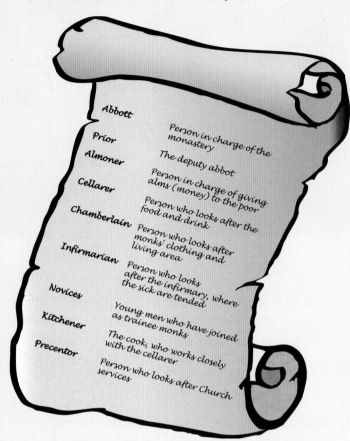

Abbott — Person in charge of the monastery

Prior — The deputy abbot

Almoner — Person in charge of giving alms (money) to the poor

Cellarer — Person who looks after the food and drink

Chamberlain — Person who looks after monks' clothing and living area

Infirmarian — Person who looks after the infirmary, where the sick are tended

Novices — Young men who have joined as trainee monks

Kitchener — The cook, who works closely with the cellarer

Precentor — Person who looks after Church services

## Stage 2: reading statements

Now read the statements on pages 111–112, which have been made by some of the monks in the monastery. As you read each statement, fill in an evidence chart like the one below.

This chart should contain the following information.

- Who has given the statement.
- The job done by that person.
- Anything suspicious arising from the statement.
- Reasons why the person might have wanted to have killed Novice John.

An example has been done for you, so you can see what type of thing you should be writing on this sheet. **WS**

| Name | Reasons for suspicion |
|------|----------------------|
| precentor | Looks after the Church services. |
| | Was the last one to see John alive. |
| | Had a candle, and there was wax found next to the body. |
| | There doesn't seem to be a motive. |

## Stage 3: using all the information you have to decide who committed the murder

Having read through all the statements and filled in your evidence chart, think about who you suspect of murdering Novice John and why. In your groups, can you agree on who committed the murder?

## Stage 4: catching the suspect

Now that you have agreed who murdered the novice monk, design a 'Wanted' poster that may help to catch him. Your poster should have:

- a big, bold heading – something like: 'WANTED FOR THE MURDER OF NOVICE JOHN'
- the name of the suspect
- the reasons you suspect this person of murder.

### The precentor's statement

*I was the last person to see Novice John alive. He seemed very unhappy the last couple of days, as if he had some terrible news. I know that his mother came to see him recently. Such a kind woman, although nobody knows who Novice John's father was.*

*I left John to lock up because he said that he wanted to stay behind and pray. So I took my candle and left. The next thing I hear, the poor boy is dead. The abbot called me straight away.*

### The abbot's statement

*I found the body after the Church service of Compline. At first, I didn't see the body because my candle was so low. It was lying at the base of the night stairs … you know, the stairs that lead directly from the living quarters into the Church. He was last out of the church because he was clearing the chapel.*

*John worked with the precentor. We haven't moved a thing at the scene of the murder. As you will see, there is a large pool of wax by his body. There are also muddy footprints leading from the body up the stairs and into the dormitory. It looks like poor Novice John was stabbed with a short knife, possibly the kind used to sharpen quills for illuminating manuscripts.*

*I don't know who would murder Novice John. He was so young and didn't have any enemies. He seemed so happy here. In fact, I can safely say that I never saw him unhappy. We live such a simple life. The monks have taken a vow of silence (apart from when praying in Church), so they communicate with each other using sign language.*

*The monks have little contact with outsiders – apart from the poor who come to the abbey to receive alms money. The monks need permission from me if they want to receive guests or travel. I am the only one who is allowed to leave the abbey without telling anyone. I have been reading the Bible to them at mealtimes this last week and didn't notice anything strange.*

### The chamberlain's statement

*My job is to look after the monks' habits and the dormitories. I saw Novice John yesterday and he was very serious. Usually he would smile a lot, and would try to tell me plenty of news using sign language. He was such a pleasant young man and he had only been here a year.*

*John had a visit from his mother a few weeks ago and ever since then his mind has been elsewhere. Lately, I have been teaching him how to illustrate manuscripts. Indeed, I have an example here of one of his pieces of work. He has learned how to sharpen quills.*

### The cellarer's statement

*I have been in charge of food and drink for the last six years. I had a busy day as always. After Prime, I had to check the ale and draw some for breakfast. I also had to make sure we had enough bread.*

*The lunch was easy – the monks had ham. In the afternoon, I caught some trout in our fish-pond and cooked it in time for supper. As always, I went out after Vespers to feed the pigs and took a stroll down to the river to visit the necessarium … you know, to use the lavatory. It's terribly muddy down there at the moment. The river was flooded for weeks.*

*Vespers was the last time I saw Novice John. I feel sorry for the Abbot. He looks so worried. A murder is the last thing he needs. In fact, he has looked worried for weeks.*

### The almoner's statement

*I was giving out alms all afternoon. It was quite busy today, but it has been all year. It is always busy when there has been a poor harvest. There has been little work with so much land under water after the floods. Then there were the usual poor from the village, including Novice John's mother. She always takes her money without saying a word.*

*After the poor had left or were in their rooms for the night, I cleaned the floors of the alms room, which were covered with mud. Then I spent an hour in the carrel, the room in which we illustrate manuscripts. After supper, I collected a candle and went to Vespers. I stayed on in silent prayer until Compline, then went to my dormitory.*

### The kitchener's statement

*Everyone liked Novice John. I can't imagine who would try to kill him. They said he was stabbed. I counted my knives, but they were all here.*

*I feel so sorry for the Abbot. He has worked very hard to make this monastery successful. I saw him yesterday down by the river cutting reeds, which we will eventually use for basket making. He must have worked several hours that day, because it was getting dark by the time he came back from the river. He wasn't in Vespers, but he often missed chapel in the evening and then prayed late.*

## Plenary

Look back at pages 106–112. In pairs, discuss what you have learned about the lives of monks and nuns. Then discuss how important you think the Church and religion were in the Middle Ages. Write out five questions you would like to ask about religion in the Middle Ages.

# WHAT AND WHO WERE PILGRIMS?

**Objectives**

By the end of this section you will be able to answer these questions.
• What sort of people went on pilgrimages?
• How did they travel to get to their place of pilgrimage?
• Why was Canterbury such a special place?
• Why did Henry II quarrel with Thomas Becket?
You will organise information and present your results.

## Starter

*At some time during their lives, many people in the Middle Ages tried to go on a pilgrimage, which is a journey to visit a religious site. The people who went on a pilgrimage were known as pilgrims. With a partner, look at Source A.*

Pilgrims on the road to Canterbury.

💡 *What types of people can you see in Source A? Try to write down ten key words to describe the scene.*

💡 *What clues are there in the picture that tell you about the kind of people going on the pilgrimage?*

💡 *Can you think of any places of pilgrimage today?*

# Sites of pilgrimage

It could take pilgrims days or sometimes months to reach their destinations. There were a number of pilgrimage sites across Europe. The most popular in England was at Canterbury Cathedral, where people would come to visit the shrine of St Thomas Becket (see pages 117–119).

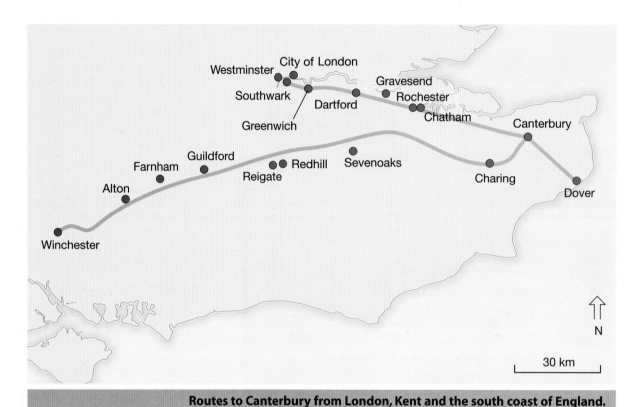

**Routes to Canterbury from London, Kent and the south coast of England.**

But people didn't only go on pilgrimages in England. Some travelled to Jerusalem in the Holy Land to visit the sites connected to Jesus' life. At these sites they would buy relics, which were religious items that people felt might bring them luck.

💡 Why do you think people went on pilgrimages?

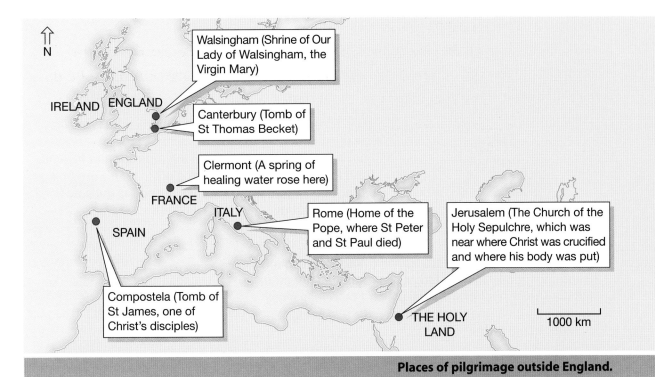

**Places of pilgrimage outside England.**

# TASKS...

1  In pairs, you are going to investigate why people went on pilgrimages. You will either produce a report in the form of a booklet or give a presentation to the class.

Your investigation should be based around questions like these:

- What kind of people went on pilgrimages?
- What were their occupations?
- Why did people go on pilgrimages?

In pairs, or as a class, brainstorm to come up with more questions to help your investigations.

2  To help you gather information, you could put your ideas on a mind map. Use the outline below to help you get started.  **WS**

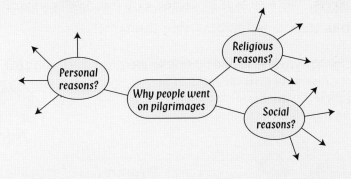

# Medieval pilgrims

So, why did people go on pilgrimage? As you read about each of the characters you will occasionally notice the name St Thomas. Remember what these characters say about him.

**Knight**

*I am a knight. I have fought all over Europe and beyond from Russia to Jerusalem. I am a noble man. I am going on the pilgrimage to give thanks to God for my safe return from war.*

*I am a squire. This means I am learning how to be a knight, so one day I can be like my father. I have already fought in wars in France, but I'm still very young. I especially enjoy drawing, dancing and singing. I am on the pilgrimage to accompany my father.*

**Squire**

**Wife of Bath**

*I am a cloth-maker from Bath. I enjoy pilgrimages. In fact, in the last few years I have been to Jerusalem twice, Rome, Compostella and Cologne. I think that going on pilgrimages to places abroad is more likely to get you closer to God. I have had five husbands.*

*I am a monk, but I don't like the strict rules laid out for monks by people like St Augustine. I enjoy the food and company on this trip. At supper last night, I ate a whole roast swan! I want to visit the holy shrines but I also like pilgrimages because they are a bit like an outing.*

**Monk**

**Friar**

*I am a Friar called Hubert. I make much of my money from begging. I like talking to the barmaids in the taverns. Pilgrimages are like nice holidays!*

*I am a nun and try to live close to God by setting an example to others. I want to visit the tomb of St Thomas to pray there. I walk beside my donkey as a way of punishing myself for my sins.*

**Nun**

**Miller**

*There are lots of us young millers on pilgrimage. I like cracking jokes and having fun. St Thomas – why is he important?*

## The struggle between the Church and the king

As you read in Chapter 2, the Church was very important in people's lives in the Middle Ages. Most people believed that God controlled everything. The Church was central to village life and everyone would go there every Sunday. People went to church to pray and to confess their sins. They feared that if they did not, they would go to hell. The Pope was the head of the Church, not the king. However many medieval kings challenged the power of the Pope and tried to control the Church themselves.

Thomas Becket was a close friend of Henry II. Henry made Becket Archbishop of Canterbury in 1162. As archbishop, Becket would have to be loyal to the head of the Church, the Pope in Rome. This led to a bitter quarrel between Henry and Becket, because Henry was angry that Becket now took the side of the Pope instead of the king.

## The death of Thomas Becket

SOURCE B

A picture of 1190 showing Thomas Becket's death.

SOURCE C

The murder of Thomas Becket, from a fifteenth-century manuscript.

# TASKS...

1    Read statements (a) to (o), which describe a quarrel between King Henry II and Thomas Becket. These statements give clues about why Becket was killed. The only problem is, the statements are not in the right order. With a partner, work out the right chronological order of the statements. **WS**

**a)** The Church was rich and had great power.

**b)** As part of his attempt to control the Church, Henry II made his friend Thomas Becket Archbishop of Canterbury in 1162.

**c)** Becket returned to England in 1170, but still refused to do what Henry told him.

**d)** In 1164 Becket was forced to go into exile in France.

**e)** Four of Henry's knights rode to Canterbury. They burst into the cathedral.

**f)** The knights shouted, 'Where is Thomas Becket, traitor to the king and realm?'

**g)** The Church had its own laws, called canon laws. King Henry II wanted to control the Church and to end its right of trying priests in its own court.

**h)** Becket even excommunicated [threw out of the Church] any bishop who took Henry's side.

**i)** Very soon Becket had become the most popular saint in England.

**j)** Pope Alexander III was horrified by Becket's murder. In 1173, Becket was made a saint and 29 December was made St Thomas' Day.

**k)** Henry's temper snapped. He cried: 'Will no one rid me of this turbulent [difficult] priest?'

**l)** Henry II also wanted the right to appoint the bishops of the Church. This would give him greater control over Church affairs.

**m)** Pilgrims began to visit the shrine of Becket. In 1174, Henry II visited the cathedral. He was flogged by the monks as punishment for the murder of Becket.

**n)** Becket appeared. The knights set about attacking him. An eyewitness, Edward Grim, wrote that they scattered his 'brains and blood about the pavement'.

**o)** Henry's appointment of Becket as archbishop backfired. In 1163, he refused to hand priests over to Henry's courts for trial.

# TASKS...

**2** Look at Sources B and C on page 117, which will provide further evidence about Becket. Think about which person in each source is Becket. List the clues that tell you what happened to Becket.

**3** Finally, discuss in pairs what you have learned about Thomas Becket and build a story of his murder.

### The importance of Becket's tomb

People were outraged by Becket's death and soon began flocking to his tomb to see his relics, because people had reported seeing miracles there. Relics could be a saint's bones, or clothing or possessions. People believed relics to be holy and visited shrines such as Becket's at Canterbury Cathedral to touch or pray before these holy relics.

# TASKS...

**1** Why do you think Becket's tomb at Canterbury was such an important shrine? In pairs, come up with as many reasons as you can.

**2** Why was Becket murdered?
  **a)** You might want to use the cards on page 118 to help you answer the question.
  **b)** When you have decided why Thomas Becket was murdered, write a catchy headline for a newspaper about his death. Think about the type of newspaper the headline will appear in. Will it be a tabloid or a broadsheet newspaper? If it is a tabloid you might want to use alliteration in your headline.

**3** Why do you think Henry II wanted to control the Church?

## Plenary

Write a one minute newsflash on the death of Thomas Becket, to present to the class. **WS**

# WHY GO ON A CRUSADE?

By the end of this section you will be able to answer these questions.
- What are the three most popular religions in the world?
- What were the Christian attitudes towards the Crusades?
- What were the Muslim attitudes towards the Crusades?

You will be able to see that there are usually at least two sides to every argument.

## Starter

### *Whose point of view is right?*

*It is natural for people to hold very strong opinions, or beliefs. However, not everybody thinks in the same way and so not everybody shares the same views about what is right and wrong. Here are some examples of things that people often feel very strongly, and differently, about:*

- *The death penalty – right or wrong?*
- *Eating meat – a natural appetite, or cruelty to animals?*
- *The role of women in society – housekeeper and mother, or career woman?*

💡 *What strong opinions, or beliefs, do you hold? Have you ever met somebody who holds the opposite point of view? How did you feel towards that person?*

*When people hold strong opinions about things, it is often very hard to find any points of agreement. In this section you will discover how people with very different religious beliefs thought about and behaved towards each other during the Middle Ages.*

💡 *Can you think of any situations in the world today where groups of people are in conflict because of the different beliefs they hold? Brainstorm and make a list.*

## The world's three most popular religions

Jerusalem is a very important city for three of the world's most popular religions.

## Key words

**Muslim** Someone who believes in the teachings of the Prophet Muhammad. His or her holy book is the Koran.

**Christian** Someone who believes that Jesus Christ is the Son of God. His or her holy book is the Bible.

**Jew** Someone who believes in one God. His or her holy book is the Tenakh.

## Islam

Jerusalem is home to the Dome of the Rock. In AD 620, the founder of Islam, Prophet Muhammad, arrived in Jerusalem. From the el-Agra stone under the Dome of the Rock in the centre of the city, Muhammad ascended to the Seventh Heaven, then returned to Makkah. The mosque that was built on the site of this miracle became the third holiest place in the **Muslim** world.

## Christianity

The hill of Calvary in Jerusalem was the place where Jesus Christ was crucified. It was from Jerusalem that he was reborn and went to heaven. Jesus also preached on the Mount of Olives in the city. From the fourth century, **Christian** pilgrims from all over the world flocked to visit the holy sites of Jerusalem and the Holy Land.

## Judaism

In AD 70, the Romans destroyed the most important temple of the Jewish faith that had been built by King David. In AD 135, the **Jews** were thrown out of the city. However, the importance of Jerusalem to the Jews as the city of King David meant that it was one of the holiest cities for the Jewish people.

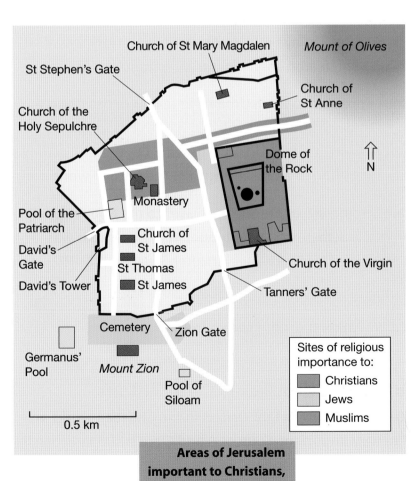

Areas of Jerusalem important to Christians, Jews and Muslims.

## Arguments about Jerusalem and the Holy Land

The city of Jerusalem and the area around it is known as the Holy Land. This area has been argued over for years by Christians and Muslims. Your aim is to find out about the different attitudes most Christians and Muslims had towards each other between the eleventh and thirteenth centuries.

## The Muslims and the Christians

Until the eleventh century, pilgrims of all religions were able to visit Jerusalem. The city was controlled by Arab Muslims. In the 1070s, Jerusalem fell under the control of the Seljuk Turks, who were also Muslim. However, the Seljuk Turks were less willing to let Christian pilgrims visit Jerusalem.

Meanwhile, across Europe, Christian armies had been defeating the Muslims in Sardinia, Spain and Sicily. In the eleventh century a large area of central and southern Europe was known as the Byzantine Empire. The Byzantines, led by Emperor Alexius Comnenus, were afraid of the Seljuk Turks and feared they might try to conquer their land.

In 1095, Alexius appealed to Pope Urban II as leader of the Christian Church for help to defeat the Muslim Turks in both Europe and Jerusalem. At Clermont in 1095, Urban II appealed to the Christian world for help in fighting in a Crusade against the Muslim world.

Crusaders came from all over Europe in answer to the Pope's appeal. The most famous British person who fought in the Crusades was Richard I (Richard the Lionheart – see Chapter 5, pages 146–152).

- 💡 Have you heard the word Crusade before?
- 💡 Where do you think the word comes from?
- 💡 What do you think people were fighting for?

## Pope Urban II's attitudes

The Pope was the most important person in the Christian world, and his views were very important. Sources A and C are by Pope Urban II. Source B shows Christian attitudes towards the Muslims.

# TASKS...

1   In pairs, look at Sources A, B and C. Pick at least five key words or phrases from these sources that tell us about Christian attitudes towards the Muslim rule of Jerusalem. You can put these words on a chart like the one below.

|  | Keywords and phrases to describe source |
|---|---|
| **Source A** |  |
| **Source B** |  |
| **Source C** |  |

## SOURCE Ⓐ

A horrible race has violently invaded the lands of the Christians. They have destroyed the churches of God and even changed them into churches for their own religion. Jerusalem is now the prisoner of the enemies of Jesus Christ. These people don't even know how to pray to God. Everyone going to fight to free Jerusalem will be forgiven their sins.

**Pope Urban II speaking in 1095.**

## SOURCE Ⓑ

**A thirteenth-century illustration showing Christian attitudes towards Muslims.**

## SOURCE Ⓒ

I know that many of you have heard about the wild attacks of the Muslims against Christian churches. They have even made a slave of the Holy City of Jesus, Jerusalem.

**Pope Urban II writing in 1096.**

# The Crusades

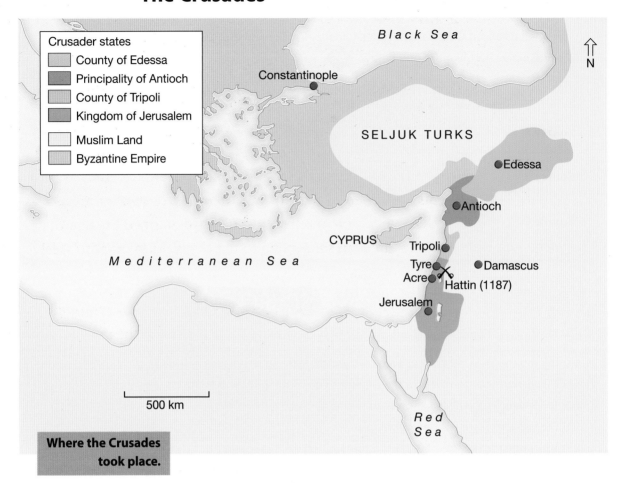

**Where the Crusades took place.**

The next 300 years saw a number of attempts by Christian armies to conquer Jerusalem and dominate the Holy Land.

### The First Crusade

The first Crusade started in 1096 and lasted three years. It was a success for the Crusaders, but only after two years of hard fighting. Many areas of land between Constantinople and Jerusalem came under Christian rule. By the end of the First Crusade, only half the number of knights who had originally set out had returned.

### The fight for the city of Jerusalem

The biggest success of the First Crusade for the Christian armies was the capture of Jerusalem. However, when the Crusaders first arrived in Jerusalem they had to wait three weeks for their siege equipment to arrive before they could begin their attack. Also, the defending Turks had planned for a long siege and had stored up lots of food within the city walls, so that the Crusaders had little food to survive on.

The Christian attack on Jerusalem was a fierce one. Christian archers fired arrows. Steel hooks attached to long ropes were catapulted onto the city walls, in order to pull the walls down. Huge battering rams with iron-capped heads were used to break down the city gates. Boulders were rolled into the moat so that the Crusaders could cross.

The defending Turks resisted the attack on their city with energy. They used bales of straw to withstand the shock of battering rams. They threw pots of 'Greek fire' over the walls onto the Crusaders. These pots contained a burning liquid made up of sulphur, resins and oils which exploded on impact. The Turks also dragged the dead bodies of the Christian soldiers on to the city walls, in order to steal their weapons and armour.

It was a month before the Christian invaders finally broke through the city walls. Once inside, buildings were burned to the ground, precious goods were stolen, and some 70,000 Turks and Jews were murdered. The Crusaders now claimed Jerusalem as a Christian city.

💡 What do you think the people of Jerusalem would have thought of their new Christian rulers?

***The struggles between Muslims and Christians continue …***

Between 1096 and 1291 there were six different Crusades, but none of them acheived the success of the First Crusade. Terrible violence was committed on both sides, and the hatred and distrust between Muslims and Christians deepened. However, there were also times of peace when Muslims and Christians tolerated and even became friendly towards each other.

**The Crusades continue …**

1145–9    The Second Crusade. The Crusaders lose control of many areas of land they had won during the First Crusade.

1187    Saladin, the leader of the Muslims in Egypt, defeats the Christian armies at the Battle of Hattin and goes on to conquer Jerusalem.

1189–92    The Third Crusade. Led by Richard I of England and King Phillip of France, the Crusaders capture Cyprus and Acre but fail to take Jerusalem.

**1202–4** The Fourth Crusade. Christian armies attack and destroy Constantinople. However, the Crusaders are criticised as being selfish because the crusade is more about winning trade routes than religious belief.

**1217–22** The Fifth Crusade. The leaders of this Crusade fail to take Jerusalem.

**1228–9** The Sixth Crusade. The Holy Roman Emperor makes an agreement with the Sultan of Egypt and the Christians retakes Jerusalem.

**1244** The Crusaders are thrown out of Jerusalem by the Muslim leader as-Salil Ismail.

**1291** The Crusaders leave the Holy Land.

## The Children's Crusade

It was not just adults who were involved in crusading. In 1212, hundreds of French and German children decided they would go to the Holy Land and recapture Jerusalem from the Muslims. They believed they did not need to be armed, because God would look after them.

The German children reached Pisa (in Italy), and the French got to Marseilles from all over France. They both hoped for ships to take them to the Holy Land. The German children set sail, but were never heard of again. The French children were tricked by two Christian merchants, Hugh Ferreus and William Porcus. These merchants packed the children on to seven ships and set sail not for the Holy Land but for the slave markets of Alexandria in Egypt. Two ships were lost at sea. The children who survived the journey across the Mediterranean were sold as slaves.

## TASKS...

1 Working in pairs, one of you will take the role of a Christian child, the other a Muslim child. Now write a speech explaining to each other your different attitudes towards the Crusades.

In your speech you should try to argue for your religion. You should use persuasive language to try to convince others of your opinion. Remember to write in the first person.

## SOURCE D

During the siege of a town, one of the European women came to us asking to see Saladin. She said that her daughter had been taken in the night by Muslims. Tears came to Saladin's eyes. He sent a horseman to the local slavemarket to look for the girl. They both returned not long after. The girl's mother threw herself to the floor with emotion.

**Adapted from Baha ad-Din Ibn Shaddad writing at the time about Saladin.**

## Different views

Look again at Sources A, B and C on page 123. Then study Sources D to H, which are all written or drawn by Christians and Muslims.

## SOURCE E

As soon as one of our knights, Lethold, climbed the wall of the city, the defenders ran away. Our men chased them, killing as many as they could until they were up to their ankles in blood. When our men captured the Temple, they killed whoever they wished. Soon our soldiers took the whole city, and seized gold, silver and houses full of treasure. The dead Muslims were piled up high outside the city and their bodies burned.

**Adapted from the Christian story _Deeds of the Franks_, written by an unknown author. He was in Jerusalem in 1099 when the Crusaders took the city.**

## SOURCE F

**This picture reflects one aspect of Muslim culture. Here you can see a garden in Baghdad where rich men are being entertained.**

## SOURCE G

### Key words

**Pagan** A person who does not believe in any of the major world religions but worships the natural world.

The land where Christ was born has fallen into the hands of **pagans**. The bodies of saints have been fed to animals and our churches have been turned into stables. Those of you who join up to free the land of Christ's birth from the pagan will be granted a place in heaven by God.

**Pope Celestine III speaking in 1195, encouraging Christians to fight in the Holy Land.**

WHAT WERE PEOPLE'S BELIEFS IN THE MIDDLE AGES?

127

SOURCE H

Jerusalem is our Holy City from where the Prophet Muhammad made his miraculous journey. On Judgement Day, when we meet Allah [God], our people will be united there. We do not want to give it up to the Frankish beasts who are only interested in conquering land and riches.

**By a Muslim writer in the twelfth century.**

# TASKS ...

1  In pairs, look at all the sources in this section. Now pick at least five key words or phrases from each source that tells us about Muslim attitudes towards the Holy Land and the Crusaders. You can put these words on a chart like the one below.

| | Keywords and phrases to describe source |
|---|---|
| **Source A** | |
| **Source B** | |
| **Source C** | |
| **Source D** | |
| **Source E** | |

2  Now that you have learned about the attitudes of the Muslims and Christians, discuss in groups of four why people from these two religions had such different viewpoints. One person in the group should make a note of the ideas you come up with. Each group could then tell its conclusions to the whole class. Here are the some questions you might like to discuss.

💡 How do the Christians and Muslims differ in their attitudes towards the Crusades?

💡 Why do you think they had such different attitudes?

💡 Do you think they were sometimes inaccurate in their views?

💡 What can we learn about the Crusades that is relevant today?

## Plenary

Do you think that people with different beliefs can exist peacefully together? How is this possible?

# DID PEOPLE OF THE MIDDLE AGES BELIEVE IN THE SUPERNATURAL?

Objectives

By the end of this section you will be able to answer these questions.
- Did people believe only in God?
- What else did people believe in?

You will do an activity to draw together what you have learned about beliefs in the Middle Ages.

## Starter

*There are several important questions we might ask ourselves in life. Why do you think storms happen? Why does the moon eclipse the sun? Why does it occasionally hail? Why do animals catch diseases? Do UFOs exist?*

SOURCE A

**Do UFOs exist? How can we know for certain?**

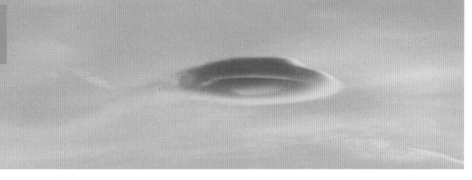

*It is possible to find out answers to the first four questions. But we really don't know the answer to the last one. People have lots of suggestions about UFOs. Some think they are hoaxes (a joke). Others think they may have something to do with strange weather patterns.*

*When people don't know the answer to a question, they sometimes blame the 'supernatural', because it is very difficult to explain what the 'supernatural' is and to prove it exists.*

💡 *Can you think of a story or event you have heard or read about recently that people believe was caused by the supernatural? Write down briefly what the story is.*

## The powers of the Church

In medieval times, things in the natural world that people did not understand were explained as the works of God (who was represented on earth by the Church). You have already read about the pilgrimages to Canterbury (see pages 114–119). Many pilgrims hoped that by visiting Becket's shrine they would be cured of certain illnesses. The Church explained the supernatural in a number of ways.

- The work of saints – those people considered most holy were made saints and people offered prayers to them in the hope of being cured of illness or protected from harm.

- Church rituals – things done by priests and other Church people on a regular basis.

- Superstitions and charms – actions involving some aspect of the Church that people felt might bring them luck, improve their lives or protect them. This was different from magic that was the work of the Devil.

## The power of Saints

Stories of saints were very popular during the Middle Ages. People also learned about the good deeds and the miracles of saints through paintings, statues and stained glass windows in church.

Each saint had his or her own symbol and area that they could influence. People would pray to a particular saint depending on their current needs and fears – for example, St Christopher was thought to protect travellers and so people prayed to him before going on a long journey. Each saint had a special day in the church calendar when feasts and celebrations remembering their life were held. People would flock to a shrine if a saint's body was buried there.

### *Miracles*

Saints were said to have achieved miracles during their lifetime. For example, St Foy de Conques was believed to have cured blindness. It was thought that miracles were possible because of a person's holiness. In the Middle Ages, people prayed to saints in the hope that they had the power to bring miracles into their lives.

💡 Who do you think would make a modern saint? Can you think of a public figure who sets a good example to us all?

💡 Can you think of anyone who has achieved a modern miracle?

## Rituals and relics

### Rituals

Rituals were another way in which medieval people thought that they could get closer to God. These symbolic acts or practices were carried out on a regular basis, to mark a special occasion or particular form of worship. They ranged from simple actions, such as kneeling during prayer or the clothes that priests wore, to more complex events, such as religious plays and periods of fasting.

💡 Some tennis players must always bounce the ball a certain number of times before they play a point, to bring them good luck. Do you think this is a 'modern ritual'? How is it like a medieval ritual, and how is it different?

💡 Do you carry out any 'modern rituals' in your life? Or do you know of anybody else who does?

### Relics

Relics were objects which had belonged to a saint. They might be the saint's clothes, hair, nails, or even their bones! These objects were thought to bring you closer to the power of the saint, and so people would travel many miles to visit a Church where a relic was housed. Pilgrims would pray to a relic, but touching a relic was even better! Relics were believed to have special powers to perform miracles such as healing.

# TASKS...

1 Using resources in your classroom or the Internet, do some research to find out about a medieval saint, ritual or relic. Write a short report to feedback to the class. When writing and presenting your report, remember to:
- State the facts about what you are talking about. You could use the 5Ws – who, what, when, where and why – to help you structure your report.
- Say what was special about that saint, ritual or relic.

# TASKS...

**2** You are going to answer the key question, *'What were people's beliefs in the Middle Ages?'* Divide a double page in your exercise book into four equal squares. In each quarter, write some information about what people believed in. You will need to identify four key beliefs. You could include the following information for each belief:

- What was the belief about?
- How did people behave as a result of this belief?
- Why did people have this belief? (For example, you might want to think about the teachings of the Church, religious stories or religious practices.)

Can you think of any other information you could find out about each belief? **WS**

## Plenary

Did you think any of the beliefs from the Middle Ages were ridiculous? Which ones? Why did you think this? How might you explain this to a person from the Middle Ages?

# WHO WAS THE BEST AND WHO WAS THE WORST KING, 1087–1307?

## 5

## TIMELINE
## 1087 to 1307

**1087** William the Conqueror dies. His son, William Rufus, becomes King of England.

**1100** William Rufus dies. Henry I is made king.

**1106** Henry I gains control of Normandy.

**1120** William and Robert, Henry's sons, drown at sea.

**1135** Henry I dies leaving the throne to his daughter, Matilda. It is also claimed by his nephew, Stephen of Blois, who becomes king.

**1154** Henry II becomes king.

**1162** Henry chooses his friend Thomas Becket as Archbishop of Canterbury.

**1170** Becket is murdered in Canterbury Cathedral.

**1189** Richard I is made king.

**1199** John is crowned king.

**1215** King John is forced to sign the Magna Carta.

**1216** Henry III becomes king at the age of nine.

**1265** First Parliament meets.

**1272** Edward I becomes king.

**1307** Edward I dies.

The rulers of England in the Middle Ages were very powerful. But what kind of people were they? Until Edward I, who is the last king we will look at in this chapter (see pages 157–8), most kings considered themselves Norman or French as much as English. Their first language was French and they spent much of their time France. This was because they had lots of land in France, which they had got by conquering it or through marriage.

Ruling England after 1066 was not an easy job. It was especially difficult for William I because he had conquered the country and many people didn't accept him as king.

*You have already read about William the Conqueror's reign in Chapter 2. What difficulties did William face as king?*

Look at the family tree on page 134 to see who the kings of England were between 1087 and 1307.

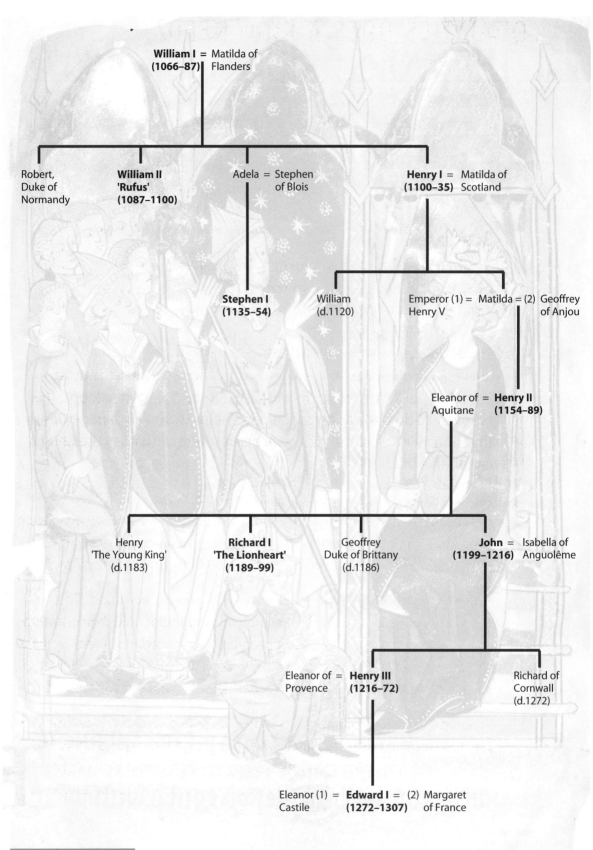

William I = Matilda of
(1066–87) Flanders

Robert,
Duke of
Normandy

William II
'Rufus'
(1087–1100)

Adela = Stephen
of Blois

Henry I = Matilda of
(1100–35) Scotland

Stephen I
(1135–54)

William
(d.1120)

Emperor (1) = Matilda = (2) Geoffrey
Henry V          of Anjou

Eleanor of = Henry II
Aquitane     (1154–89)

Henry
'The Young King'
(d.1183)

Richard I
'The Lionheart'
(1189–99)

Geoffrey
Duke of Brittany
(d.1186)

John = Isabella of
(1199–1216) Anguolême

Eleanor of = Henry III
Provence     (1216–72)

Richard of
Cornwall
(d.1272)

Eleanor (1) = Edward I = (2) Margaret
Castile        (1272–1307)    of France

# WHAT QUALITIES DOES A KING NEED?

**Objectives**

By the end of this section you will be able to answer these questions.
• What makes a good king and what makes a bad king?

You will also be investigating:
• What are the important factors for being a good king?

### Starter

*Write down five things that you think make a good king. You can simply make a list of these things, or you can do them as a spider diagram. Compare what you have written with others in your class.*

### Important factors for being king

Ruling England in the Middle Ages was a complicated job. The most important thing a monarch had to do was keep hold of the throne. The best way to do this was to stay on good terms with important groups in the country. Three of the important groups were the barons, the Church and the people.

A good English king in the Middle Ages was one who could keep the peace. But medieval kings also needed to be good in war. They needed to keep their large amount of land in France, deal with neighbours close to home in Scotland, Wales and Ireland, and end any uprisings at home.

A good English king also needed to provide good government. This means that the country had to be run well and the people didn't have to pay too many taxes. Many good monarchs introduced new ideas to make the country run even more smoothly. For most of the people, the best rulers would deliver peace and prosperity, be fair and not too violent.

To keep the peace, a guaranteed successor – such as a son – was useful because it would give stability to the king's reign. If everyone knew and agreed who was going to be the next monarch, it would stop people arguing about it or putting themselves forward. If rivals to the throne appeared, then they had to be dealt with effectively.

So it is clear that medieval kings needed to have strong personalities. They also needed some luck. Some kings are seen as being good because they were lucky enough to rule in times of peace and prosperity. Others might have been good if they had ruled in less troubled times.

💡 Jot down the difficulties facing medieval kings. Which do you think would have been the hardest to deal with?

# TASKS...

**1 a)** Get into groups. On a large sheet of paper, copy out the list below. Then discuss whether the things on this list make a king good. Remember that everything on the list is important, but some things are more important than others.

- Protected the empire.
- Dealt effectively with neighbours.
- Had a male heir who could take over as king.
- Had peaceful relations with the Church.
- Good with the country's money.
- Good at administration of the country.

- Difficulty with the barons.
- Had a strong personality.
- Had few challenges to the throne while king.
- Engineered peace and prosperity.
- Successful in war.
- Few popular rebellions against him.

**b)** Look back at your own list or spider diagram. Add your own points to the sheet you have already started. If more than one of you in the group has made the same point, you only need to write it on the sheet once.

**2** On your own, think about six things on the list that are more important and six things that are less important in making a good king. Now try to explain to the rest of your group why you have made your choice. Listen to what others in the group have chosen.

**3** As a group, draw a chart like the one below. Agree on which six things are more important and which six things are less important, then add them to the chart. **WS**

| More important factors | Less important factors |
|---|---|
|  |  |

If you prefer, you can put these things on a line with the more important factors on the top and the less important factors below.

You are now ready to begin working on your answer to the key question: *'Who was the best and who was the worst king, 1087–1307?'*

## Plenary

What qualities would you find in a really *bad* king? Make a list. Try to think of at least five qualities

# WILLIAM RUFUS OR HENRY I: WHICH KING WAS BETTER?

By the end of this section you will be able to answer this question.
- Who was the better king, William Rufus or Henry I?

By examining the sources, you will be able to:
- compare the reigns and reputation of William Rufus and Henry I
- come to a final decision about who was the better king.

## Starter

*Look at Sources A and B. Why do you think that William's nickname was Rufus? (Here's a clue: the word 'Rufus' describes an aspect of his looks.)*

💡 *What else do you think Source A tells us about William Rufus?*

💡 *What does Source B tell us about Henry I?*

William Rufus, who was King of England from 1087 to 1100.

Henry I, who was King of England from 1100 to 1135.

## William Rufus

William Rufus got his name because he had red hair, and lots of it! He also had a terrible temper and would shout at everyone around him. Many people were frightened of William. Yet when they came to write about him, they were very kind.

Peter of Blois, whose account you will read in Source C, didn't much like William Rufus. But were Peter's criticisms of William fair? Peter of Blois might not have liked William Rufus, but on page 139 you might find enough things about William that you think make him a good king.

William Rufus was William I's second son. When William I died in 1087, his eldest son, Robert, was given Normandy. William Rufus was made king of England. The third son, Henry, was given £5000.

💡 Do you think that William I treated his three sons fairly? Give reasons for your answer.

## Henry I

Henry I did have some advantages over his brothers. He was born in England, whereas the other two were born in Normandy. This meant he could argue that he was English, but his brothers were French. He spoke English as well as French. When William Rufus died in 1100, Robert should have been made king, but he was on a Crusade in another country. By the time he came back to England, Henry, his younger brother, had made himself king.

## TASKS...

1  a) In pairs, read Source C. As you read, pick out five to ten words or phrases that show what Peter of Blois thought about William and his followers. Write them down. **WS**

  b) Now read Source D. Again, as you read, pick out five to ten words or phrases that show what Peter of Blois thought about Henry I. Write down these words or phrases. **WS**

  c) With your partner, discuss which of the two kings you think Peter of Blois preferred. How can you tell this from the two sources? What does this tell you about looking at language used in sources?

SOURCE C

William Rufus ruled with a powerful arm and brought all of his opponents under control. In 1088 he crushed the revolt of barons in Normandy, and in 1095 he crushed an attempt to replace him with Robert. Soon there was no one who dared to plot against him, even though many people felt that his rule was harsh and unfair.

William had no respect for the Church or religion and became an enemy of the Pope. In 1097 the Archbishop of Canterbury, Anselm of Bec, was so fed up with William Rufus's bullying, he went to France. William made his friend, Ranulph, the Bishop of Durham. But Ranulph was an unpopular, greedy crook who helped William get every penny he could out of the Church and the people in taxes. The worst thing was that William and Ranulph spent much of the money they stole on having fun.

These were bad times in England. Thunderstorms with violent winds shook towers of churches and brought them to the ground. On the earth there were fountains flowing with blood and mighty earthquakes. There were a number of murders. There was a famine, and an outbreak of disease so great among men, as well as animals, that agriculture nearly collapsed.

Abroad, William got control of Normandy in 1096. He even managed to conquer more bits of France – including the regions of Maine and Vexin. He made good relations with the kings of Scotland and Wales.

In the end he was killed in a hunting accident by a man called Walter Tirel, who aimed an arrow at a stag. It missed the stag and pierced the king in the breast. The king fell to the earth and instantly died. Some countrymen carried his body back to the palace in a cart. Few people were upset at William's death. He died without an heir.

**Adapted from Peter of Blois, a Frenchman writing about William Rufus in the thirteenth century.**

SOURCE D

Henry, who was better educated and cleverer than his two brothers, succeeded William on the throne. His eldest brother, Robert, was away crusading so missed his chance. Anyway, Henry was better suited to being king. Straight away he gave freedom to the Holy Church, and issued a Charter of Liberties that promised fair rule. He also threw William's friend, Ranulph, into prison and asked the most holy Archbishop Anselm to come back from exile. However, Ranulph escaped to Normandy and encouraged Robert (who had recently returned from the Holy Land) to invade England. Robert raised a large army, and landed in England in July 1101. But there was no fighting. Anselm got the two sides to agree and set peace terms.

• Robert should return to Normandy and give up his claim to the throne.
• Henry should pay an annual compensation of £3000 of silver.

However, Robert stopped taking this annual payment and plotted against Henry. In 1106 Henry invaded Normandy, defeated his brother's army and kept him in prison, where he died. Normandy was united with his own kingdom. This was quite expensive and sometimes Henry had to raise taxes to fight to keep Normandy. In 1118 he fought against the king of France and his allies, who tried to snatch Normandy from him.

In 1107 Henry made peace with the Church by giving up the right to appoint people to Church positions. But he kept some control over the appointment of bishops. This, I think, was the right thing for Henry to do. Anselm was known for causing trouble. So when he died in 1109 Henry did not replace him as Archbishop of Canterbury.

These were good times. England was run very well. Henry set up new ways to run the country. Royal courts were seen as fair and honest. The country was doing so well that many people came to England from Normandy. In 1128, some monks arrived who set up a programme of road building and improving the land.

In 1100 Henry married a Scottish woman, Matilda, who was very popular with the people because she was not French. Henry and Matilda had four children – two boys and two girls. But tragedy struck this family. The two sons, William and Robert, were drowned in 1120. Henry chose Matilda to be his heir. She was married to a Frenchman called Geoffrey Plantagenet. By the end of his reign, Henry was quarrelling with Matilda and Geoffrey. Matilda had a rival who also wanted to claim the throne – her cousin, Stephen of Blois. So the reign of Henry I did not come to a happy end.

**Adapted from Peter of Blois, writing in the thirteenth century, on Henry I.**

# TASKS...

1 You have made your decision about which king Peter of Blois preferred based entirely on what he wrote about the two men.

   **a)** What do you think are the problems of making a decision based on the views of one person?

   **b)** Do you think you can trust what Peter of Blois says? Give reasons for your answer.

## Plenary

Now that you have completed the task on page 138, it's time to make up your own mind about who you think was the better king – William Rufus or Henry I. Copy a spider diagram like the one opposite. Choose who you think is the better king and fill in the five things you think are better about this person.

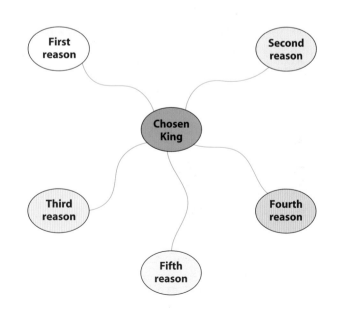

# STEPHEN OF BLOIS OR HENRY II: WHICH KING WAS BETTER?

**Objectives**

By the end of this section you will be able to answer this question.
• Who was the better king: Stephen or Henry II?

By examining the sources, you will be able to spot:
• what is fact (something that is true; something that actually happened)
• what is opinion (the view of one person).

You will also be able to:
• assess the reign and reputation of Stephen I and Henry II
• compare the two monarchs and come to a final decision about who was the better king.

## Starter

*In groups, brainstorm to come up with a list of five monarchs. Are they all kings? Or have you included any queens? Do you think only men make good monarchs? Give reasons for your answer.*

**Stephen of Blois, who was King of England from 1135 to 1154.**

## Stephen of Blois

William Rufus and Henry I were brothers, but they were very different. On pages 139–40 we read what happened at the end of Henry I's reign. He decided that Matilda (his daughter) would become the next ruler of England.

💡 Why do you think a female monarch might have been a problem for many of the nobles?

Stephen of Blois was very unhappy about Matilda becoming queen. His mother, Adela, was Henry I's sister, which he thought gave him more right to the throne.

Stephen's desire to become king led to a **civil war**. Some barons supported Stephen and other barons supported Matilda. When Henry I died in 1135, Matilda was in France. So Stephen crowned himself king. This was very underhand, especially as Stephen had sworn to support Matilda the previous year. His reign lasted until 1154.

The civil war had a very bad effect on England. Barons began to do what they wanted, such as building castles and seizing land. The Scots invaded the north of England, and took over the counties of Cumbria and Northumbria. The Church also became more powerful and sometimes had a greater say in affairs than the king himself.

Stephen had a son called Eustace, whom he wanted to be his successor. However, Matilda felt that her son, Henry, should become king after Stephen. Unfortunately for Stephen, Eustace died.

In 1153, the Archbishop of Canterbury, Theobold, helped Stephen and Matilda to come to an agreement. Matilda would recognise Stephen's right to be king, and Stephen would recognise Henry as his successor. A year later, Stephen died and Henry was crowned Henry II.

## SOURCE B

Henry II, who was King of England from 1154 to 1189.

## Henry II

Henry II was King of England from 1154 to 1189. He married Eleanor of Aquitaine, which gave him plenty of French territory to add to his empire, as you can see from the map on page 143.

Henry was a thick-built man. He was well educated, but had a terrible temper. Henry had several sons, but his favourite was John. However, his sons rebelled against him towards the end of his reign, which made him even angrier.

Henry is often remembered for an argument he had with Thomas Becket. In this argument, Henry wanted Thomas to agree to allow priests who had broken the law to be tried in his courts, not in Church courts.

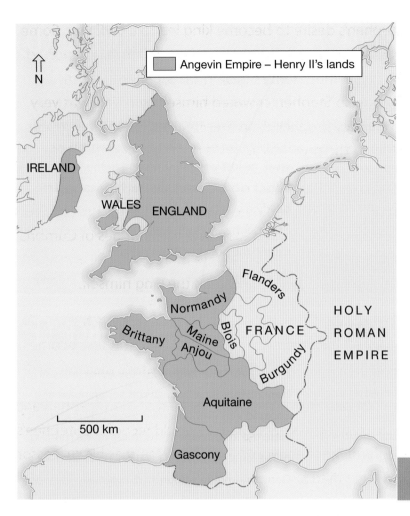

Angevin Empire – Henry II's lands

IRELAND

WALES ENGLAND

Flanders

Normandy

Brittany Maine Blois FRANCE

Anjou

Burgundy

Aquitaine

Gascony

HOLY ROMAN EMPIRE

N

500 km

**Henry II's empire during his reign as king.**

Thomas was the Archbishop of Canterbury, the most important churchman in England, so he felt strong enough to refuse Henry's request. In 1170, Henry flew into a rage, and four of his knights rode to Canterbury and killed Becket in Canterbury Cathedral.

But it's not fair to remember Henry just as a bad-tempered king, he also made improvements to how the law courts worked and to government taxation.

# TASKS...

1 Working in pairs, look at Sources C to F. WS

a) One of you will read Sources C and D, which are about Stephen of Blois. The other should make a list of five questions to ask about Stephen. When you have both finished, try to answer the five questions. Write down the answers.

b) Now swap jobs! The person who wrote the questions about Stephen will now read Sources E and F. The person who read Sources C and D will now make a list of five questions to ask about Henry. When you have both finished, try to answer your five questions. Write down the answers.

c) Now compare the answers you have for Stephen of Blois with the answers you have for Henry II. Discuss which king seems to be the better of the two. Write down your choice and be prepared to justify your answer.

## SOURCE C

In the days of Stephen, there was nothing but chaos, civil war and robbery. The barons of the country rose up against him. When they found out that Stephen was a mild mannered, happy-go-lucky man who would not punish them, they committed many crimes. This chaos lasted for the whole time Stephen was king, till the country was in ruins.

**Adapted from the *Anglo-Saxon Chronicle* written in the twelfth century.**

## SOURCE D

All of Stephen's reign was overshadowed by war. In 1141, his army was defeated by Matilda's forces. But she was so unpopular that the people would not allow her to be crowned. Stephen was so weak, he lost land in France, and to the Scots and Irish. One bright point was that his reign saw the building of lots of new churches and monasteries. However, he was even weak in letting the Church extend the power of Church courts.

**A modern historian writing about Stephen.**

## SOURCE E

Henry is honest in speech, has good table manners and is generous. Our king is a peaceful man, but victorious in war. He works very hard and is always trying to improve how the country is run.

Henry has added to his empire by being strong in the Duchy of Normandy, the duchy of Brittany, the kingdom of England, the kingdom of Scotland, the kingdom of Ireland and the kingdom of Wales. No one is kinder to the sick and ill, no one friendlier to the poor, no one more unbearable to the proud. The death of Becket was a mistake, but it was because Henry wanted to bring justice to the Church.

**Adapted from a description of Henry II by Peter of Blois, written at the time.**

## SOURCE F

Henry II restored England to the good times of Henry I. The Great Council was set up again and England was well governed. Especially important were the improvements he made in the running of the legal system and taxation. Trade with Germany and Italy flourished, especially the wool trade. There was only one revolt in 1173–4, and that was easily crushed. He introduced strong English rule in Ireland in 1172 and made the Welsh recognise the power of the English crown.

**A modern historian writing about Henry II.**

It is important to think about facts and opinions all the time when looking at sources. If you think something is a fact, you might be able to trust it more. If you think it is an opinion, you need to find out more about the author in case he or she has twisted the evidence.

# TASKS...

1  In pairs, look again at Sources C to F.

   **a)** One of you will choose three facts (something that is true) from these sources and will explain to your partner why you think these things are facts. When you have both agreed that they are facts, write them down.

   **b)** Now swap jobs! One of you should choose three opinions (someone's view) from the sources and explain why these things are opinions. When you have both agreed that they are opinions, write them down.

## EXTENSION TASK...

2  Working in pairs, use the information you have gathered about Stephen and Henry to design book covers for the following titles:
   - *The Reign of Stephen of Blois*
   - *The Reign of Henry II.*

   You will design one cover each. Remember to use a picture or several pictures that clearly show the key features of your king's reign. As you design your cover, think about the message you want to put across. Was your king a good person? Was he a bad person? Make a feature of anything on your cover that highlights this. Your cover should include both facts and opinions about your chosen king.

   When you have completed your cover, show it to your partner and explain your design. Then let your partner explain his or her design.

## Plenary

If you were going to make a Hollywood blockbuster about Stephen of Blois and Henry II, which actors would you choose to play them? Which key event from each of their lives would you use in your film? Why?

# RICHARD I OR JOHN: WHICH KING WAS BETTER?

**Objectives**

By the end of this section you will be able to answer these questions.
- Have historians been too kind to Richard?
- Did John really deserve his bad reputation?
- Who was the better king: Richard or John?

By examining the sources, you will be able to:
- assess the reign and reputation of Richard I and King John
- compare the two monarchs and come to a final decision about who was the better king.

## Starter

*In this section we will be looking at two kings, one who is remembered as being a good king, and one who is remembered as being a bad king.*

*Think about someone famous – someone who you do not know personally. Do they have a good or a bad **reputation**? What has the person done to get that reputation? Do you think they deserve to be thought of in that way? Give reasons for your answer.*

*Feedback your results to the rest of the class. Now see if you can together answer the following question:*

*Does a person always deserve their reputation?*

## Richard I and John

**SOURCE A**

A contemporary portrait of Richard I, who was King of England from 1189 to 1199.

When Henry II died in 1189, his eldest surviving son, Richard, became king. In films and TV programmes about Robin Hood, Richard is shown as being a good and brave king. His nickname was 'Richard the Lionheart'. However, the truth about Richard is not quite so clear. He spent much of his time abroad fighting in the Crusades.

💡 Why do you think Richard I was known as Richard the Lionheart?

Richard's brother, John, who was king from 1199 to 1216, has been given a different image. His nickname was 'Lackland', because he wasn't given any land by his father.

Which king, John or Richard, do you think has a good reputation? Which king has a bad reputation? Why do you think this?

**A contemporary portrait of King John, who was King of England from 1199 to 1216.**

# TASKS...

**1  a)** Look at Sources C to F, which are pictures about Richard I and John. Study them carefully. They provide evidence that will help you to decide who you think was the better king. The notes below will also help. **WS**

**Stage 1: thinking about sources in general**

When thinking about sources, we need to consider the following.

- Nature – what type of source it is (for example, a painting, a drawing, a letter, a poem and so on).
- Origin – who produced the source and when.
- Purpose – why this source was produced and for whom.

**Stage 2: how to study pictures**

When looking at pictures you need to ask certain questions.

- What is the person who drew or painted the picture trying to show?
- Was the person who drew or painted the picture there at the time?
- Is the person who drew or painted the picture trying to make things up?

You might want to hypothesise or speculate about the pictures by asking questions such as: 'Why was this picture drawn?' (In other words, what is its purpose?)

Try to make links between the pictures you see and your own knowledge to make up your mind about them.

**b)** With a partner, try to find answers to the questions above for each source.

**c)** Now discuss whether these sources can be used as evidence to help us decide who was the better king. If you don't think they can, explain why.

# Richard I and King John: the evidence in pictures

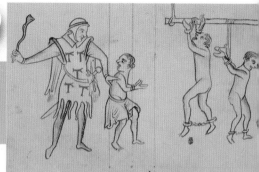

A picture of one of John's officials, drawn by a monk called Matthew Paris, who wrote about John in 1235.

SOURCE D

From the *Lutterell Psalter*, showing Richard I jousting with his enemy Saladin. The truth is that these two men never met.

SOURCE E

A medieval painting called 'The flight of Richard the Lionheart from the armies of Philip Augustus'.

## SOURCE F

**A modern artist's impression of John signing the Magna Carta.**

# TASKS...

**1  a)**  Look briefly at Sources G to O which are things that historians have written about Richard I and John. They have been taken from a range of history text books. They provide evidence that will help you to decide who you think was the better king. **WS**

Remember when reading written sources you need to ask certain questions. Look back at page 147 to remind yourself of these questions.

**b)**  On a page in your exercise book, write the heading: 'Richard and John – the main issues'. Then look more carefully at these sources. As you read each source, make a note of the key words to show the main issues of Richard's and John's reigns. Try to sum up each issue in three of four words, which you can add to your list. An example has been done for you. **WS**

Richard and John: the main issues

| | |
|---|---|
| Source G | Relations with the Church. |
| Source H | |
| Source I | |

# Richard I and King John: the written evidence

Richard didn't argue with the Head of the Church, the Pope. This wasn't surprising, as he spent most of his time fighting for the Church on the Crusades. John's big mistake was that he argued with the Church and the barons at the same time. The Pope and John argued over who should be Archbishop of Canterbury. In 1207 the Pope insisted Stephen Langton was given the job, but John refused. In 1208 the Pope shut down England's churches. The following year he threw John out of the Catholic Church. In 1213 John had to apologise and give in to the Pope's demands.

**A modern historian's opinion of King John and Richard the Lionheart.**

When king, Richard I only visited England twice. Both times he came simply to raise more money for his wars abroad – especially the Crusades and wars against Phillip II of France. By the time Richard died, he had made England a poor country.

**From a modern history textbook.**

Richard had little to do with Wales, Scotland or Ireland. However, John married his daughter, Joan, to the Welsh prince, Llewelyn the Great.

**From a modern history textbook.**

John married Isabella of Angouleme, who had been promised to a French nobleman, Hugh of Lusignan. Hugh was very angry and complained to the French king, Philip II, who declared war on John. John's armies were defeated by the King of France in 1204 (after which he lost Normandy) and 1205 (when he lost Anjou). His hopes of getting back his land were destroyed when his army lost again to the French at the Battle of Bouvines in 1214.

**A modern historian's account of John's reign.**

**SOURCE K**

When Richard was away, the country was run well by Hubert Walter, who was, among other things, Archbishop of Canterbury. Knights living in England were given more responsibility in day-to-day government when the king was away fighting abroad.

**A modern historian's comment on changes during the reign of Richard I.**

**SOURCE L**

Richard died without an heir, but John had several children – including a son called Henry. However, John was not particularly kind to all children. There is a suspicion that he had his nephew and rival to the throne, Prince Arthur, put to death.

**From a modern textbook.**

**SOURCE M**

In 1192, Richard was returning from the Crusades when he was taken prisoner by one of his enemies, Duke Leopold of Austria. He was kept prisoner for two years, until he bought his release in 1194 using £100,000 of tax money raised in England.

**From a modern textbook.**

**SOURCE N**

When John came to the throne, England was a poor country. His brother, Richard, had spent all its money. John's problem was that he hadn't been very successful during all his years at war, so many barons complained about the high taxes he made people pay. In fact, John made the barons he didn't like pay even higher taxes. War broke out between the barons who supported John and those who hated him. In the end, the barons that hated John forced him to sign the Magna Carta in 1215. The Magna Carta aimed to protect their rights.

• No taxes (known as scutage) could be asked for without the permission of the barons.
• Nobody would be imprisoned without first having a fair trial.
• The barons would meet in a Great Council to advise the king.

After signing the Magna Carta, John made it clear he was forced to agree to these conditions, and he persuaded the Pope that it should be ignored. Civil war broke out again in 1216, but then John died.

**A modern account of the troubles faced by King John.**

Richard was a great soldier and a great crusader. Indeed, he led the Third Crusade. He did what all great kings at the time had to do.

**From a modern textbook.**

# TASKS ...

**1** What was the Magna Carta?

**2** How do you think it changed the relationship between the king and the barons?

**3** In groups, look at the key issues you have raised on your charts or in your exercise books. Now discuss who dealt best with the main issues, Richard or John.

**4** Write an extended answer to the question: *'Who was the better king, Richard or John?'* Use the information you added to your issues chart to help you with this. You may like to look back to Chapter 2 (page 73), which will give you some help with this writing.

## Plenary

Consider all the different things you have learned on pages 146–152 about Richard I and John. In groups, discuss whether you think the reputations of Richard and John are accurate.

Now think of two new nicknames – one for each king. Discuss in your groups why you think they are appropriate.

# HENRY III OR EDWARD I: WHICH KING WAS BETTER?

**Objectives**

By the end of this section you will be able to answer this question.

• Who was the better king – Henry III or Edward I?

By examining the biographies and sources, you will be able to:

• assess the reign and reputation of Henry III and Edward I

• compare the two monarchs and come to a final decision about who was the better king.

SOURCE A

## Starter

*Take a look at Sources A and B. Who do you think is more powerful today – the Queen or Parliament? Give reasons for your answer.*

**Queen Elizabeth II, the current Queen of the United Kingdom.**

SOURCE B

**The British Parliament today.**

*In this section you will find out about a big fight that broke out between the king and Parliament during the Middle Ages over who had power.*

## SOURCE C

## Henry III

Henry III and Edward I both had long reigns. But for many, that is where the similarity ends. Henry was king from 1216 to 1272, and his son Edward ruled from 1272 to 1307. Both men had very different personalities. Henry was religious, and considered himself more French than English. He also had to deal with the problems left by his father, which included the powerful barons. Edward, his son, was clever and energetic. His nickname was 'Longshanks' because of his long legs!

**Henry III, who was King of England from 1216 to 1272.**

## TASKS...

**1** Read through the biography on pages 155–6, which is about Henry III. As you read, jot down what you think are the eight most important events of his reign. Don't forget to make a note of the dates of these events.

**2 a)** In your exercise book, write out a timeline for your eight dates. Put the date first, then write a sentence explaining what happened in that year. **WS**

**b)** Now give each event a score. Your scores can be in the range of +5 for a very positive event for Henry to −5 for a disaster. Using crosses, plot your events onto a graph like the one opposite. When you have plotted your events, draw a line that links all the crosses. **WS**

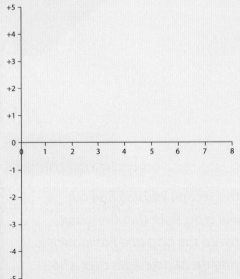

## The life of Henry III

Henry III became king in 1216 at the age of nine. For the next eleven years, he was told what to do by his guardians – William the Marshall and Hubert de Burgh. From 1227, he was old enough to rule without the help of others.

The years that followed were not easy for Henry. He was not very popular because he surrounded himself with French friends – such as his tutor and close adviser Peter des Roches. Henry had a very good relationship with the Church, but was unpopular when he gave the top jobs in the Church to foreigners. He also spent lots of money building churches. This building programme was paid for by raising the ordinary person's tax.

One of Henry's problems was that he was not very successful at fighting wars. In 1229, he fought for Aquitaine, an area to the south of France, but lost. He was defeated again in 1242, when he tried to win back Gascony from the French king. He didn't have much luck with his neighbours either.

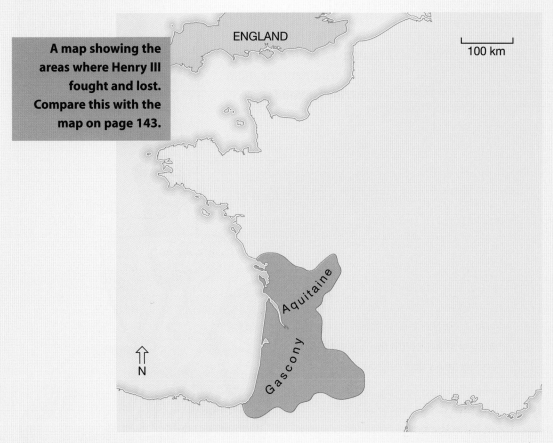

A map showing the areas where Henry III fought and lost. Compare this with the map on page 143.

Henry's wars cost too much money. This money came from increasing taxes, which didn't please the barons. In 1254, Henry promised to give the Pope money in return for appointing his son, Edmund, as King of Sicily. This was too much for the barons, and they decided to push for government reform. Led by Simon de Montfort, Earl of Leicester, the barons met in Oxford in 1258. By the Provisions of Oxford they agreed to limit Henry's power.

- A council of fifteen elected members would advise Henry. They could veto his decisions. This meant that Henry could not make decisions without the barons' agreement.
- Taxes would be decided locally, not by the king.
- Reforms would be made to the royal household, and foreigners banned.
- The king, as well as his officials, had to take an oath of loyalty to keep to the Provisions.

💡 How do you think Henry would have felt about the Provisions of Oxford?

By 1261, Henry had had enough. He decided that he would ignore the Provisions of Oxford and, in 1263, civil war broke out with Henry and his son Edward leading one side and Simon de Montfort leading the other. Simon de Montfort had the upper hand for about two years. During that time he set up a Parliament. This was a meeting not just of barons, but also some ordinary people who did not have a title like 'duke' or 'earl'. This was a very important event, because before the setting up of Parliament, the main people to give advice on how to rule England were only nobles and barons.

💡 What difference would it have made having ordinary people in a Parliament? Would they have wanted different things to the nobles and barons?

Simon de Montfort was beaten at the Battle of Evesham in 1265, and in 1267 the civil war ended. It was not such a great victory for Henry. The real ruler from now until his death in 1272 was his son, Edward.

SOURCE **D**

Simon de Montfort .

Edward I, who was King of England from 1272 to 1307, seated with bishops and monks.

# Edward I

Edward I let Parliament make more decisions than his father. He needed Parliament to be friendly, because he fought a number of wars in England and abroad.

### Why did Edward go to war against the Welsh?

During the reign of Henry III, some Welsh leaders claimed that Wales should be free from English rule. The leaders of this movement were Llewelyn, who was the Prince of Wales, and his brother David. In 1278, they started a war against the English. Edward eventually crushed the independence of the Welsh and in 1282 Llewelyn was killed in battle. In 1284, Edward's fourth son, Edward, was born in Caernavon Castle in Wales. He was given the title Prince of Wales.

### Why did Edward go to war against the Scots?

Edward I also went to war against the Scots. After the death of the Scottish monarch, Margaret, in 1290, there was no clear successor. The Scottish nobles asked Edward to choose their king. In 1292 he chose John Balliol. Many Scots did not like the fact that Edward was interfering so much in their affairs, so in 1295 the Scots turned to France for support. Edward was very angry and sent an army which defeated a Scottish army at the Battle of Dunbar in 1296. A Scottish lord, William Wallace, continued the fight against Edward and defeated the English army at the Battle of Stirling in 1297. But Edward won through, and by 1304 Scotland had been conquered and brought under the control of the English king.

### Why did Edward go to war against the French?

Edward was not so involved in affairs in France, although he had land there to protect from the King of France. In 1294, 1296 and 1297, Edward led expeditions to France to regain Gascony. None of these expeditions was successful. But the French king gave it back anyway in 1303, because he had other matters to deal with.

SOURCE E

### Why did Edward argue with the Pope?

Edward also argued with the Pope. In 1296 the Church in England would not grant Edward money as it had done previously, because the Pope, Boniface VIII, told it not to. Edward showed how unhappy he was about this by seizing church land. Eventually, the Church backed down and he got his money.

### Edward and Parliament

During his reign, Edward improved how Parliament worked. In 1295 he called a Parliament that was to represent more social groups than ever before – from bishops to townspeople. However, all was still not well for Edward. The barons and many merchants did not like having to pay high taxes, and in 1297 they made Edward agree to the Confirmation of Charters. These charters said that Edward could not raise taxes without agreement from Parliament. But Edward did not try to weaken Parliament's powers. During his reign it met regularly. There was prosperity in England, partly because Edward encouraged it – for example, in 1303 he gave merchants the right to trade freely.

## TASKS...

1  Read through the information on pages 157–8, which is about Edward I. As you are reading, jot down what you think are the eight most important events of his reign. Don't forget to make a note of the dates of these events. **WS**

2  a)  As you did for Henry III, write out a timeline for your eight dates. Put the date first, then write a sentence explaining what happened in that year.

   b)  Now give each event a score. Your scores can be in the range of +5 for a very positive event for Edward to -5 for a disaster. Using crosses, plot your events onto a graph like the one you did for Henry III (see page 154). Now draw a line to link all your crosses. **WS**

3  According to your graphs on Henry III and Edward I, whose reign seems to have been a greater success?

## Plenary

Imagine if the Queen had total power over the running of the country today and there was no Parliament. How would life in England be different? **WS**

# WHO WAS THE GREATEST KING OF THEM ALL?

**Objectives**

By the end of this section you will be able to answer this question.

- Who was the best king – William Rufus, Henry I, Stephen of Blois, Henry II, Richard I, John, Henry III or Edward I?

You will do some activities in order to make a decision about who was the best king of all. You will also assess how good all the other kings were and decide which king was the worst of all.

# TASKS...

1 Working in groups, you will act as judges to determine who you think was the best king.

a) Before you begin, make a list of all the monarchs you have studied in this chapter. For each monarch, think how well they performed in each of the following categories.

- Protected the empire.
- Dealt effectively with neighbours.
- Had a male heir who could take over as king.
- Had peaceful relations with the Church.
- Good with the country's money.
- Good at administration of the country.

- Successful in war.
- Few popular rebellions against him.
- Difficulty with the barons.
- Had a strong personality.
- Had few challenges to the throne while king.
- Engineered peace and prosperity.

b) Now give each monarch a mark, according to how well that person performed in that category. You should award marks according to the following criteria.

| 9 or 10 marks | Outstanding in this area. |
|---|---|
| 7 or 8 marks | Has performed very well in this area. |
| 5 or 6 marks | Has done a good job. |
| 3 or 4 marks | Has not done so well, but is not a disaster. |
| 1 or 2 marks | Is close to a disaster. |
| 0 mark | A disaster! |

Award 5 marks if there is no information about a category, or if that category is not relevant to the monarch you are judging.

# TASKS...

**The 'lucky' mark**

Some kings were luckier than others because they became king at a good time. Other kings inherited a bad situation. Therefore you can give the kings a 'luck' mark – 5 meaning you feel they have been very unlucky and 0 meaning they have been fairly lucky.

The monarch with the highest score is the winner!

Gook luck!

2   The class decides!

  **a)** Each group in the class should nominate their best king and explain why they have chosen this person.

  **b)** Vote for your favourite king. You can vote for any of the kings. You do not have to vote for your group's nominee.

  **c)** Collect the votes together and now you will have an answer to the key question: *'Who was the best and who was the worst king, 1087–1307?'* **WS**

3   In your exercise books you will write a commendation (a note of praise or recommendation) for the best king and the runner-up. The commendation will have the title 'Best king from 1087 to 1307'. You should draw a picture of the king in question, then write four points or more points explaining why he is the best or the runner-up.

## EXTENSION TASK...

4   Look again at the scores your own group produced for each monarch. Think about the king who scored the fewest points. Write a school-type report on the worst king. In your report, explain why you think he is the worst king of them all. **WS**

# WHAT WAS LIFE LIKE IN THE MIDDLE AGES?

## 6

*In this chapter we will be looking at the quality of everyday life in the medieval period. In many ways, this depended upon who you were and the position you held in society. The pace of everyday life in the medieval period was much slower than the pace of life today.*

💡 *Many people think that the pace of life at which we live today is very fast. What do you think they mean by this, and what could we change to make life slower? How would your life be different if the pace at which you lived was slower?*

*For people in the medieval period, life was very different from life today. So the things that they considered important to a happy life were probably quite different. However, the ability to live a secure and happy life would have been just as important to them as it is to you today.*

💡 *Based on what you already know about the Middle Ages, can you think what would have been important to a medieval person living a secure and happy life?*

Not everything about life in the Middle Ages would have been different to life today. The decisions medieval people had to take in order to make a living were very similar to the kinds of decisions people make today.

- "How do I earn a living?"
- "What can I buy?"
- "What can I sell?"
- "What skills do I need?"
- "Who else do I need to consider?"
- "What am I allowed to do?"

- "When can I say what I think?"
- "Where am I allowed to go?"
- "What can I do to improve my standard of living?"
- "What laws do I need to obey and why do I need to obey them?"

Before you start this chapter, choose some of the questions you have just read and write down some answers in rough. When you finish this chapter come back to the answers and see if, by understanding about people in the past, you can or need to alter some of your original answers.

# WHAT WAS IT LIKE TO LIVE IN THE MIDDLE AGES?

By the end of this section you will be able to answer these questions.

- How did people in the Middle Ages live?
- What were the different lifestyles people had?
- How important was a person's position in society?

You will investigate how people in the Middle Ages:

- viewed each other
- spent their days.

## Starter

*We live in very different times to the people of the Middle Ages. There are lots of things we feel are so important we can't do without them. What makes you happy or contented?*

*Make a list of ten things that you feel you could not be happy without. Compare your list to that of two or three others in your class. Have any of you written the same things? If so, make a list of these.*

'Was everyday life in the Middle Ages hard?'

## Day-to-day life

These days, not everyone is a millionaire, or lives in a big house or is able to buy the finest things. Some people find living from day to day very hard. People in the Middle Ages were just the same – some people had more than others. Look at the evidence on the next few pages from three different lives – the king (Sources A to C), the lord of the manor (Sources D to F), and the peasant (Sources G to I). You might want to look back at the diagram of the feudal system on page 59 to remind you of society's structure.

# The king's life

### His work

When William, Duke of Normandy, conquered England in 1066, it was important that he was able to *show* he was in control as well as *say* he was in control. After being crowned on Christmas Day 1066 in London, he began to build castles all over England. The Tower of London, shown in Source A, was the first of these castles.

Building castles was a way of showing the Anglo-Saxon nobles who had ruled England before him that he now controlled the country. For William himself, life had its problems. He always knew some people would disagree with him and take any chance to overthrow him.

SOURCE A

The Tower of London, William the Conqueror's first castle.

### His home

By medieval standards, the king's everyday life was very comfortable. A king would have lived in the best home, as Source B shows. It was important that the king was seen to have the best. Only people of great importance and huge wealth could afford such surroundings, and as the years passed and the king's wealth increased, so the way that he lived also changed.

The Great Hall shown in Source B went thro[illegible]ges. At the time of the conquest it would have been normal [illegible]y as 150 people to eat with the king, with food being prepared nearby to make sure that it was hot. In later years, the king separated himself and his family by sitting on a raised platform at the end of the hall. As castles became better built, kitchens were moved away from where the lord ate to avoid smells, and the king would eat in his own private rooms with just his family and invited guests.

Tapestries would be hung on the wall or over windows to give colour and some protection from draughts. Using glass to make windows would have been too expensive – even for a king – so the heavy tapestries had an important use.

SOURCE B

**The Great Hall, Penshurst Palace, Kent.**

The king would also have had the luxury of a garderobe (a basic toilet). This would simply be a hole in a bench, with the waste falling outside of the castle away from where people in the castle were living.

### His food

The king would only have eaten the best that was available, as Source C shows.

Food for a royal family of eight and all their servants at Kings Langley in 1290. This menu doesn't list any bread, vegetables, fruit, herbs and spices or pastry used in the meals.

*A FEAST DAY*
*Half a cow*
*1 and a half calves*
*1 sheep*
*1 pig*
*Half a wild boar*
*2 kids*
*6 chickens*
*12 pigeons*
*450 eggs*

*A FISH DAY*
*200 salt cod*
*300 herrings*
*3 conger eels*
*5 smoked eels*
*576 ordinary eels*
*1 pickerel*
*13 and a half litres of oysters*
*Whelks*
*Trout*
*Salmon*

## TASKS...

1  Look at Sources A, B and C, which give evidence of what it was like to be a king in the Middle Ages. Now write down some key words that describe the king's life.

SOURCE D

We made frequent movements around the different Paston manors, holding court, collecting rents, seeing to the upkeep of buildings, and checking on the activities of the bailiffs, reeves and lesser servants.

**The work of a Lord of the Manor. From a modern history book.**

## The lord of the manor's life

### His work

The lords, who ruled on behalf of the king when he was away, had many luxuries. But their lives were still not as comfortable as the king's. The lords who governed in the shires (counties of England) and owned several areas of land had been tough soldiers at the time of the Norman Conquest. The work of a lord was different to the work of the king, as Source D shows.

### His home

As Britain became more peaceful after the Norman Conquest, there were changes in the way that people lived. The lord of the manor no longer needed a fortified (strengthened) castle. Instead, he was able to live somewhere much more comfortable. The castle in Source E shows some of the early changes being made at the end of the thirteenth century.

Although the castle still had its defences – like a moat, gatehouse and tower – the rest of the building was designed for living a life of some luxury. The rooms were smaller and the windows bigger. To block draughts, the windows were fitted with glass. It was difficult to produce in large quantities, and was therefore only used by the rich.

Apart from one large hall, there were lots of smaller rooms, which the family and its guests could live in. These rooms were separate from where the many servants would work and live. The castle was built to have rooms with only one purpose. Bedrooms and kitchens were placed at each end of the building. The large outside courtyard was used to entertain. It was also an area to prepare defences, if necessary.

## SOURCE E

**Stokesay Castle, built in the late-thirteenth century.**

### His food

The lord of a manor could not eat as richly as the king. But it was expected that the manor house could show its wealth by being able to lay on fine banquets for special occasions. The death of a lord was marked by a grand meal at which invited guests celebrated his passing, as Source F shows.

The Paston servants had been working for days killing beasts, brewing beer, and cooking geese and chickens. The guests also consumed 1000 eggs, 20 gallons of milk, 41 pigs and 49 calves.

**Description of a meal eaten at the funeral of John Paston in 1466.**

## TASKS...

1 Look at Sources D, E and F, which give evidence of what it was like to be a lord of the manor in the Middle Ages. Now write down some key words that describe a lord's life.

2 Compare these words with the ones you listed for how a king lived at this time.

## SOURCE G

At Cuxham in Oxfordshire in 1086, the seven most prosperous peasants had individual holdings of twelve acres. In return for them, they owed services: providing a man to work on the lord's demesne on alternate days throughout the year, two extra men at harvest time; ploughing and harrowing a quarter acre of demesne; and at Christmas, giving the lord 6d or a cock, two hens and two loaves of bread.

**A description of the work that a peasant often had to do for the lord of the manner, in addition to his own work. An extract from a modern history book.**

## The peasant's life
### His work

For a peasant in a village, life would be very different to that of the king or his lord. Work on the land was the most important part of a peasant's life. The type of work a peasant did depended on the season. According to the time of year, he would plough, sew seeds, harvest his crops or repair his property and equipment.

A peasant did not own his own land. Instead, he would pay money to the local lord to rent a piece of land, and he would also help the lord on his **demesne**, as Source G shows.

### Key words

**Demesne** The land that a lord kept for himself.

### His home

At the end of a day's work, the peasant would come home to a building very different to that of a lord of the manor or the king. He would live in a cottage, which would probably have just one room. The only light in the cottage would come from his shuttered windows (no glass here!). The beaten earth floor would be covered in rushes to give some warmth and comfort. And it would soon get dirty from rotting rubbish. There would be a fire in the middle of the room. But poor ventilation made the room smoky. At night time, the family animals would be brought inside the cottage for protection.

An artist's impression of what a peasant's home in the Middle Ages would have looked like.

### His food

Everyday meals for the peasant and his family would be meagre. Source I describes the typical diet for one working adult.

1–1.5 kg of bread

1.5 litres of ale

Vegetable stew

0.08 kg bacon or a herring (not every day)

Details of an ordinary worker's daily food intake.

# TASKS...

1. Look at Sources G to I, which give evidence of what it was like to be a peasant in the Middle Ages. Write down some key words that describe a peasant's life.

2. Compare these words with the ones you listed for:
   a) the king
   b) the lord of the manor.

We had beef, four calves, two half sheep, a breast of veal, five lambs, six pigs, seven rabbits, eggs, butter, milk and cream, pepper, vinegar, cloves, sugar dates and honey.

**A villager lists the food given by a lord to help everyone celebrate a saint's day.**

## Feast days

Feast days were special occasions when the lord of the manor might give food to everyone in the village, as Source J shows.

# TASKS...

1. Look again at Sources A to I, which give evidence of what life was like for the king, a lord of the manor and a peasant. Now draw a mind map like the one below, then fill it in to show what you think it was really like to live in the Middle Ages. **WS**

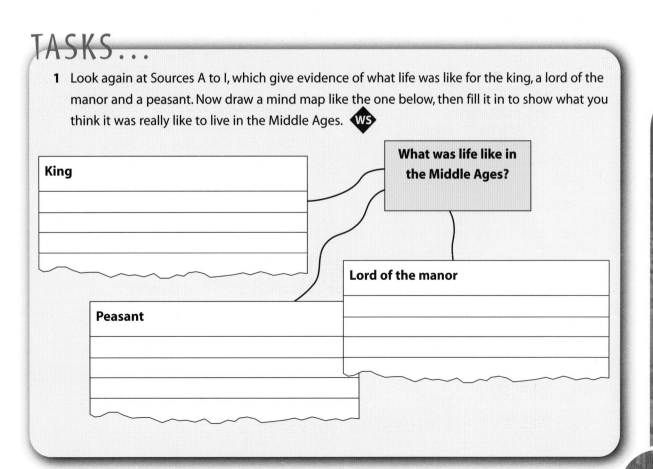

**What was life like in the Middle Ages?**

**King**

**Lord of the manor**

**Peasant**

## The law

Most of the time during the Middle Ages, people had to follow strict laws. In Chapter 2, you learned about the feudal system, which allowed the people who ruled to hold on to their power.

# TASKS...

**1** Look at statements (a) to (f) below. Some of them contain facts (things that actually happened), and some of them contain opinions (people's views).

(a) 'Ploughmen, oxherds, cowherds, shepherds, dairy workers and other keepers of animals should eat and drink as is fitting their rank, and not too much.'

(b) 'In Boldon, each villein has to pay four shillings a year and work three days a week for the lord.'

(c) 'Almost everything peasants needed had to be made at home or by one of the villagers. Every village had a blacksmith, a carpenter and other people who had special jobs.'

(d) 'I work hard all year, so that I can give my lord the service he is due and the taxes he demands.'

(e) 'Tenants should pay rent in the form of cash labour or produce.'

(f) 'People like the Pastons, who come from peasant stock, have done well to lift themselves out of the mire.'

Now draw a chart like the one below, then fill it in to show which of these statements you think are facts and which are opinions.

| | Fact | Opinion |
|---|---|---|
| Statement (a) | | |
| Statement (b) | | |
| Statement (c) | | |
| Statement (d) | | |

# TASKS...

2  **a)** Get into groups. Discuss how you each decided which statements are facts and which are opinions.

   **b)** Now look at each other's charts. Do you all agree on which statements are facts and which are opinions? If there are any differences, try to agree as a group whether this statement is a fact or opinion.

   **c)** Look again at the six statements. Who do you think would have thought these ideas?

## Plenary

Look back at what you have discovered on pages 162–170 about life in the Middle Ages.

💡 Get into groups. Your group should choose either the king, the lord of the manor or the peasant, with each of you writing your own list of five things you think would make that person happy.

💡 Look at what the others in your group wrote about this person. List the things that are the same on all your lists.

💡 Remember the lists you made at the start of this chapter about what makes you happy (page 162)? What were the main differences between things on these lists, and the things you wrote for your person in the Middle Ages?

# WHAT WAS LIFE LIKE IN THE COUNTRYSIDE?

**Objectives**

By the end of this section you will be able to answer these questions.
- Why did the people want to rebel against the government?
- What problems did the rebelling people face?
- Why did the government act as it did?

You will also investigate:
- the problems peasants faced
- the decisions that people had to make in a crisis and how they felt about those decisions.

## Starter

*We come across rules everyday – especially in school. Mostly, we keep to these rules. But sometimes there is a good reason for breaking them.*

*Why do you think we need rules? Make a list of the rules in your school. Underline the ones that you think are the most important. Then say why they are important. Think about some occasions when you might break these important rules. Make a note of your reasons.*

*Create a spider diagram to show rules that you think everyone should follow. What do others in your class think? Who do you think should make rules, and who are rules made for?*

## What happened after the Black Death?

In 1348, England was not a happy place. The country was hit by a plague called the Black Death (see Chapter 3, pages 76 and 81–2), which killed almost half the population. Peasants who survived the disease soon found that their lords needed workers to look after the crops that were rotting in the fields. Many peasants demanded, and got, higher wages for the work they did. Life did get better for ordinary families.

For the lords, things were very different. Since the Norman Conquest, life had been comfortable in many ways. The lords had land, which had been given to them as a reward for helping William the Conqueror in 1066. This land had given them wealth, power and influence.

When it came, the Black Death plague was a great shock. Not only had many people died, but also the great estates had been left with too few workers on the land. The lords of the manors, who had expected labourers to work for them out of loyalty, now faced demands from their workers for higher wages and even the freedom to work for other people.

By 1351 the government had had enough. It said peasants should know their position in the country. As a result, the government introduced a law called the Statute of Labourers, which said that peasants should not be paid any more than they were paid before the Black Death.

## Statute of Labourers

*The king knows that peasants are refusing to work without high wages.*

*– It is commanded by the king –*

- *all workers should work for normal wages*
- *workers not willing to work will be put in prison.*

**The Statute of Labourers, introduced in 1351.**

The peasants hated the new law because it stopped them from working for whoever paid them the most. However, it was not until 25 years later that events really became unpleasant. In 1377, the ten year-old king Richard II came to the throne. Four years later, he faced an angry mob of people who were demanding changes to the laws of the country.

King Richard needed money to fight a war against France. He decided to introduce a new tax that everyone over the age of fourteen would have to pay. People called it a head tax, or 'poll' tax. Whether you were rich or poor, you each had to pay exactly the same sum of money.

The peasants were angry. They went from village to village calling people to protest against the tax. In fact, in 1381 a tax collector called Thomas Brampton was lucky to stay alive when he tried to collect the tax from the people living in Brampton (a village in Essex).

The rebel peasants soon found two leaders – Wat Tyler and John Ball. Ball was a priest who said that all men were equal to each other. This was a very popular message with the peasants.

John Ball addressing the peasants in 1381.

The peasants decided to revolt. Together, thousands of them marched on London to challenge the king and his advisers. When they got there, houses of some of the rich people were burned and some advisers were murdered.

King Richard took the decision to meet the rebels and their leader, Wat Tyler, at Smithfield. The king went surrounded by his advisers. But at the meeting, Tyler drew a dagger and was killed by the Mayor of London. The king acted quickly. He told the peasants they should go home and that he would grant their demand to be set free.

The peasants went home, but the king later changed his mind about freeing them. Instead, he tracked down leaders of the rebellion and had them hanged. The heads of John Ball and Wat Tyler were placed on spikes on London Bridge (by the Tower of London) as a warning to others who wanted to rebel against the king.

The king had been angry with the peasants. He said: 'Peasants you were and peasants you are still. You will stay as slaves, except now things will be much harder for you.'

# TASKS...

1  Why do you think ordinary people were so angry they wanted to challenge the king? List six reasons.

2  Now share your reasons with a partner. Add to your list any new reasons that you come up with together.

3  King Richard told the peasants that they would 'stay as slaves'.
Draw a chart in your book like the one below.

| The lords | The peasants |
| --- | --- |
|  |  |

Write down as many words as you can think of to describe how the two groups would have felt about King Richard's words. Try to avoid the word 'angry' on either side of your chart.

4  Do you think the king made the right decision? Explain your answer.

## EXTENSION TASK...

5  At the end of the Peasants' Revolt, King Richard said:
*'Peasants you were and peasants you are still. You will stay as slaves, except now things will be much harder for you.'*

Using the information from the tasks above and your own research, write an account of the Peasants' Revolt from the point of view of the king or a peasant. Make sure that you:
- give clear opinions
- use the information you have to support your opinions
- reflect on what you have said by writing a final comment.

You may like to look back to page 73, which will give you some help with this writing.

## Plenary

Having read this section, which rules do you think the king really wanted to keep? Who do you think should make rules? Who do you think rules are for?

# WHAT WAS LIFE LIKE IN A MEDIEVAL TOWN?

Objectives

By the end of this section you will be able to answer these questions.
- Why did people choose to live in a medieval town?
- What occupations did those people have?
- What problems did people living in a town face?

You will also investigate:
- why towns were popular
- whether people needed skills to live in a town
- the difficulties of earning a living in a medieval town.

## Starter

*Towns are busy places, with lots going on. You can generally do everything you need to in a town – shop, eat, go to the bank, visit the library, see a film and so on. Villages are generally much quieter places. Often, not many people live there and there isn't as much choice of things to do and buy as in a town.*

*Why do you think most people choose to live in a town rather than a village? In pairs, write down as many reasons as you can why people might choose to live in a town today. Compare your results with the pair closest to you. Try to put your reasons into groups, then think of titles for these groups.*

## The growth of towns

In the Middle Ages, most people lived in villages. Even after the Black Death, when many villages disappeared because the people who lived there had died, it was unusual for people to live and work in towns.

After the Norman Conquest, England became more peaceful. The population in towns began to rise, which meant an increase in the number of goods people needed. Surplus goods grown on the manorial estates were sold in the towns, and peasants would visit the towns to exchange or buy goods that they needed.

### What charters did

For the lords who controlled the land, allowing a town to grow had its advantages. The king benefited by granting a charter, which allowed towns to hold a market and, in some places, an annual fair. In return for this right, the towns paid money to the king. They also had to pay an annual tax.

A town receiving a charter, which allowed it to hold markets and sometimes fairs.

| Town | £s paid to the king |
| --- | --- |
| Boston | 1100 |
| Bristol | 2200 |
| King's Lynn | 770 |
| Lincoln | 1000 |
| London | 11000 |
| Shrewsbury | 800 |
| York | 1620 |

Tax paid to Edward III by towns in England in 1334.

## TASKS...

1  On a map of Britain, find the towns named in the tax list in Source B. How do the figures help you to understand what was happening to towns in England in this period?

The charter gave towns other rights, too. Walls with gates often protected medieval towns and the people who lived in them. Strangers who came into a town would be asked about their business there, and some would be charged tolls (payments), adding to the wealth of a town. The greater the amount of trade that happened in a town, the more money would be created and the wealthier the town would become. For this reason, those who did trade in the markets had to follow rules that protected customers. Officials, paid for by the town's council, checked to see that traders were not cheating people who bought in the markets.

### Differences between towns and villages

In villages, the people who worked there still struggled to get the things they needed to survive. But it was not the same in towns. People generally had more money to spend on things like clothes, which resulted in new trades springing up. The streets were named to show the business that took place there – such as Shoemaker's Row in Ludlow.

**This picture reveals one type of punishment that was used on traders who cheated their customers.**

In villages, there might only have been one person called Thomas from the village of Stafford, so he would be known as Thomas of Stafford. But as the number of people living in towns grew, imagine what it would have been like if you were just known as Thomas. People had to add other words to their names, so that they didn't get confused with others who had the same name. These words were often connected to the work they did. So, for example, Thomas the baker would become Thomas Baker.

## TASKS...

**1 a)** Using the example of Thomas Baker, write down the sorts of jobs you think the following people did in the Middle Ages. You may need to use a dictionary to find some of the meanings of the last names.

- Richard Cooper
- William Mason
- Peter Farrier
- Elizabeth Cartwright
- Mary Smith
- Sarah Wainwright
- John Draper
- Matilda Taylor

**b)** List any other last names you can think of that might have come from the jobs people did in the Middle Ages.

### The importance of craft guilds

Craftsmen (who had a special trade, like shoemaking) formed guilds to help protect the businesses they were running. These guilds made rules about who could work for them, how they should make their goods and the prices these goods could be sold for. There were special punishments if a member of a guild broke the guild's rules.

The top craftsmen (known as masters) in a particular trade could employ **apprentices**. These apprentices would work for low wages for seven years for their master. At the end of this time, the apprentice then had to produce a masterpiece, to show that he was a skilled worker in his trade. After this, if he had enough money he could set up his own business with his own apprentices.

As Source D shows, members of a guild also paid a small amount of money to that guild, which could then be used if they were ill or became too old to work.

### Key words

**Apprentice** Someone who is learning a trade.

If it so happens that any of the members become poor through old age, or through any other chance, through fire and water, thieves or sickness, then the member shall have one and a half pennies per week, from the common box.

**What the Tanners Guild of London did to support its members.**

On the feast of Corpus Christi, all members shall come together to the guild feast.

**Rules of St Michael Guild, Lincoln.**

Guilds also organised entertainment for the town. They would plan plays based on Bible stories. Each guild would act out a tale that suited its craft – like the ship-builders performing a play about Noah and the Flood. As well as this, guild members would dress up to have huge guild feasts, with everyone belonging to that guild attending. Source E shows that going to these feasts was part of a guild's rules.

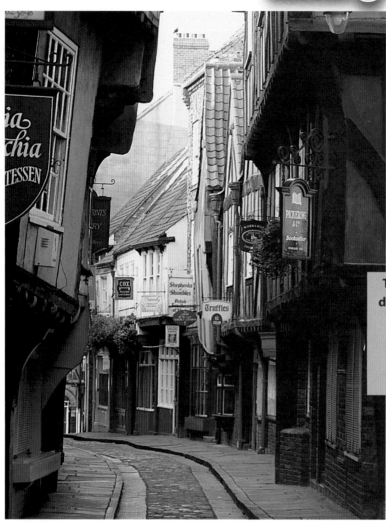

The Shambles in modern-day York. The shops would have been different in medieval times, but the layout would be practically the same.

### The town fair

Some towns had an annual fair, and this would be the highlight of the year.

The fair would last for several days, and would attract merchants and traders from a wide area, including other countries. The king would charge a town for holding a fair. So, in turn, the town would charge traders to set up their stalls and sell their goods.

When towns first started to have fairs, the stalls were little more than covered areas. But traders wanted their stalls in a place where they would be seen by the greatest number of people. Obviously, the more people who went past a trader's stall, the more chance the trader had of selling something. This led to shops developing on long narrow areas called burgage plots. These plots were permanent places on the high street, with room behind for the production of goods. Look at Source F, which shows a typical medieval burgage plot.

# TASKS...

1 Re-read pages 176–180 to remind yourselves about life in a medieval town. Remember your list of the reasons why people might choose to live towns today? Now list the differences you think there are between town life today and town life in the Middle Ages.

2 Copy out a mind map like the one below to show what life was like in a medieval town. **WS**

Draw lines between the boxed statements that seem to have a connection with each other. On the connecting line write a reason why you have connected them together. Some of the factors may well be connected to more than one other factor. Explain your connections to a neighbour, then let your neighbour explain the connections that he or she has made.

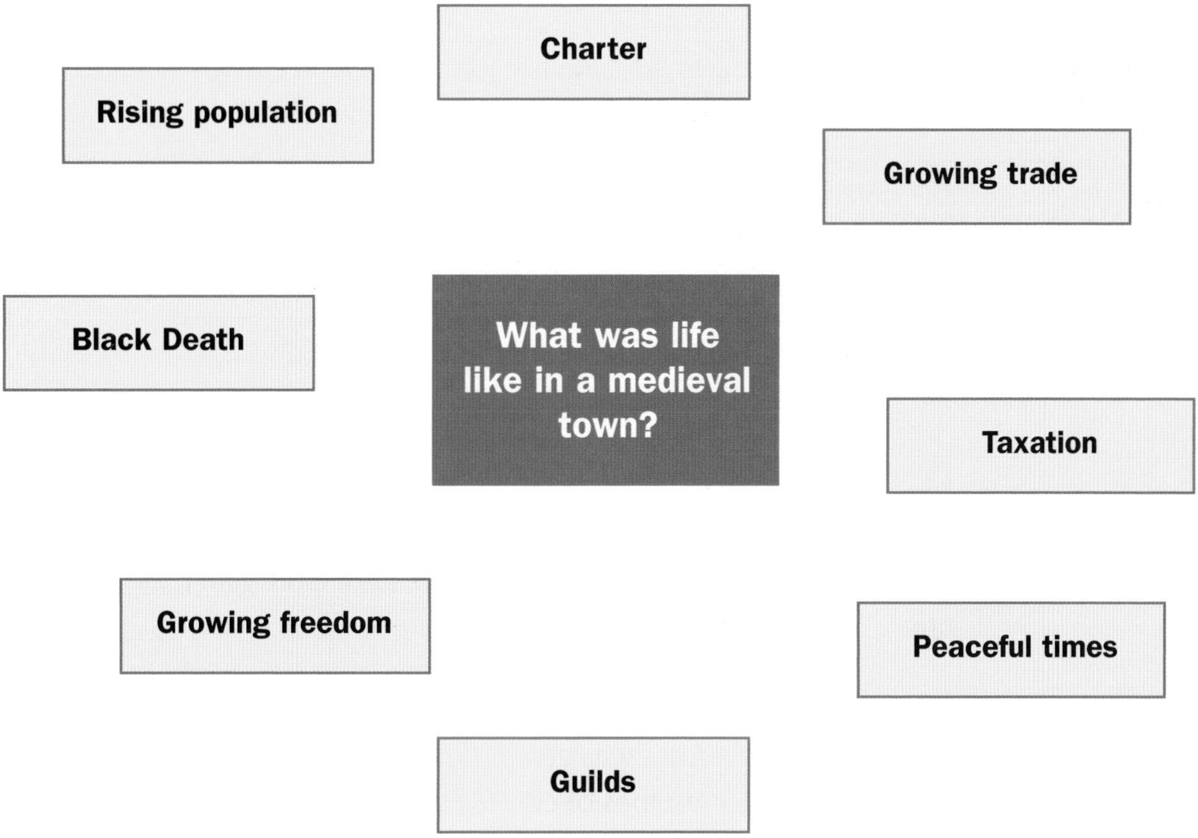

Charter

Rising population

Growing trade

Black Death

What was life like in a medieval town?

Taxation

Growing freedom

Peaceful times

Guilds

## Plenary

Look back at what you have found out about people living in a town at the beginning of this chapter. How many of those reasons were the same for people that lived in a medieval town? Are there any differences? Why do you think this is?

# HOW DID THE SYSTEM OF LAW AND ORDER CHANGE?

**Objectives**

By the end of this section you will be able to answer these questions.
• How did English law change through the Middle Ages?
• How does the law reflect the type of society people live in?
• Why did punishments change during the Middle Ages?

You will also investigate:
• the types of crimes that people committed in the Middle Ages
• how people were brought to trial
• types of punishments in the Middle Ages.

## Starter

*Every society needs to have laws, but over time laws change as society changes. Why do you think that laws change over time?*

*You have been asked to pass judgement on a person accused of stealing another person's clothes from a sports centre. Draw a three-point spider diagram and place the following questions on each point.*

💡 *What do I need to know about this case of theft?*

💡 *What methods can I use to find out if someone is guilty?*

💡 *What punishment (sentence) would I give to someone found guilty of stealing clothes today?*

*Now make notes on each of these questions. Compare your answers to others in your class.*

## Law in the Middle Ages

Law in the Middle Ages was very different to the law we have today. There were different types of courts for different people. For example, priests were put on trial in a church court. The most common court was the Manorial Court, which was run by the lord of the manor's steward (the official in charge).

The Manorial Court was very simple. Twelve villeins of the village were chosen by the village people to be jurors and pass judgement on arguments that had broken out in the village. Source A shows some examples of what they would be asked to judge.

## SOURCE A

- John Joce let Peter, a stranger, stay at his house without permission.
- Agnes, who is poor, gave birth to a child when she was not married.
- Nicholas ploughed the lord's land very badly.
- Robert owned a dog, which ate a young horse.
- Hugh dug holes in the road opposite his house.

**An extract from the Elton Manorial record.**

Jurors were not popular people. They were expected to pass harsh punishments on those who were guilty of their crimes. But the jurors still had to carry on living in the village, even though they may have made unpopular decisions about punishments.

💡 What do you understand by the word 'crime'?

💡 Who are these crimes against in the Middle Ages? Are they still crimes today? If not, why not?

### Criminals, crimes and punishments

The types of crime in the Middle Ages were very different to today. Owing money, especially to the lord of the manor, was a serious offence. People could be put in court for many things and punished in several different ways, as Sources B and C show.

## SOURCE B

| Crime | Punishment |
|-------|-----------|
| Selling rotten meat. | Put in the pillory. |
| Lying under oath. | One year in prison, but to be put in the stocks every three months. |
| Using false dice to trick people. | Put in the pillory. |
| Placing an iron in a loaf of bread. | Put in the pillory. |

**Examples of medieval crimes and the punishment that was given.**

## SOURCE C

**A pillory and a stock, used as a punishment for some medieval crimes.**

# TASKS...

1  What do you think the punishments listed in Source B are designed to do to someone who was caught?

2  Why do you think people who committed these crimes were treated in this way?

Before criminals could be tried and punished, they had to be caught. This wasn't easy in the Middle Ages. Technology wasn't used (like it is today), so you couldn't even take fingerprints, for example. 'Raising a hue and cry' was one way of catching criminals. If a villager was the victim of a crime, he would 'raise a hue and cry'. Anyone who heard the cry was honour-bound to hunt for the criminal. If they didn't, they would be fined.

Without a modern police force, different ways were tried to make sure people stayed within the law. Tithings were men over the age of twelve who formed themselves into groups of ten. If any one of the tithing committed a crime, then the others had to make sure he went to court or paid a fine for his crime. If they did not, the whole group was fined as a punishment.

## Key words

**Capital offence** A crime considered worthy of death or severe punishment.

In some cases, finding someone guilty was easy. Source D gives an example of a **capital offence**. Anyone found guilty was declared a felon and hung. But there were other ways a guilty man might be found out. One was trial by ordeal, as Source E shows.

## SOURCE D

Wakelin, the son of Ranulf, killed Matilda Day with a knife. The village, and twelve jurors, testify that he was caught in the act with a bloodstained knife, and so it cannot be denied. He is to be hanged. He had no possessions.

**Record of the trial of Wakelin, the son of Ranulf, in the eleventh century.**

## SOURCE E

Let the water be heated till it is boiling. If there is only one accusation, then let the hand dive after a stone up to the wrist. If there are three accusations, then then let the hand dive after a stone up to the elbow. Then wrap up the hand, and after three days undo the bandage to see whether the wound be foul or clean.

**Trial by boiling water, adapted from the laws of King Athelstan, AD 930. A foul wound – one that was not starting to heal – was seen as a sign of guilt.**

SOURCE F

Another way of proving guilt or innocence was trial by combat or battle, as Source F shows.

**Trial by battle, from the Hampshire Court Records, 1249.**

💡 What problems do you think medieval people would have faced in catching criminals?

💡 What do you think a 'trial by ordeal' was?

💡 Can you think of any suitable punishments for medieval crimes? Make a list.

## Justice

Look at the story below and on page 186. It is based on an event that happened in Hampshire in 1249. It's quite long. Try to remember as much as you can. You will do a task on this story later. **WS**

In Winchester in 1249, a hue and cry was raised following the disappearance of some clothes belonging to a resident of the town. Many men of the area belonging to several different tithings were rounded up and accused of the crime.

Twelve local men were quickly found to hear evidence [information to support whether someone is innocent or guilty] from those who were accused of the crime. If anyone was found to be guilty, then there could be only one verdict – as the jurors knew quite well. The value of the clothes was more than a shilling (more than 5 pence in today's money),

and because of this, any person guilty of the crime would be declared a felon. The punishment for felons was death by hanging.

The men accused of the crime were brought before the court, and the evidence was placed before the jury. It was difficult to decide who was telling the truth. Each group of men seemed to have an alibi for where they had been and whom they had been with at the time that the clothes were stolen. Justice, it seemed, couldn't be done because of the silence of some of the men, and because the twelve jurors wouldn't condemn anyone to death for so small an amount.

'I'm afraid it's a frequent occurrence in these parts, my lord, as it is throughout the country,' said one of the locals when questioned. 'Everyone needs clothes, and those who leave them lying about should know better.'

It was the answer that had been expected by the sheriff, the man presiding over the king's court. Nonetheless the clothes had gone, and the man whose clothes they were was said by all in the town to be a man of honour. Why should he lie about such a thing?

Over the next few days, different men in the village were asked different questions, until eventually one man admitted his guilt. Walter Bloweberme was known to be a rogue in the area, and with people asking too many questions he decided that honesty would be the best policy for him.

'Yes I did it,' said a shaking Walter, as the sheriff questioned him. 'But I wasn't alone and I'm not going to the gallows without a fight!'

'So who was with you?' the sheriff asked, knowing that Walter would give him the name; it was his only way to avoid the noose. 'Hamo Stare. We both did it. We broke into the house in Edeline Cross and took all sorts of things, but it was Hamo who took the coats. He said he thought they would suit him fine.' The sheriff waited. Walter was shaking with a mixture of both fear and anger.

'How do I know you are telling the truth? For all I know it could be an innocent man you are accusing.' Walter stared at the sheriff. 'If I'm lying, then let God decide,' he said, his eyes searching the sheriff's face for signs of compassion. 'I'll take Hamo on, and you'll see if I am telling the truth!'

The law of the land said that if one man was accused by another, he had the right to defend himself with his body until death or until one confessed. The sheriff looked at Walter, and slowly rose to his feet. 'So be it. Trial by battle, and may God have mercy on your soul if you are lying.'

It was not long before Hamo Stare was arrested. Told of the accusation, he denied it totally and agreed to the trial. Equipment was brought for the forthcoming conflict. Two shields at a cost of thirteen shillings and four pence; two wooden staves, each topped with a T piece sharpened at both ends; and eight shillings and three pence for their tunics of white leather and felt.

The appointed day came. Beneath a clear sky the two thieves, dressed in white, stepped out onto the field. There wasn't a large crowd, but people of the town had come to see justice done. The battle would not last long. Both men knew they were fighting for their lives, and that whoever lost would be a dead man, either on the field or on the gallows later in the day. God would decide.

The two men tore into each other, blows reigning down on the shields that they had been provided with. Within minutes it was over. Hamo, exhausted by the conflict, collapsed in a heap at the feet of his former friend, weeping like a baby.

Justice had been done. Walter had been telling the truth, and God had seen that he had won the day. For Hamo, he had just a few hours left before the gallows took his life.

# TASKS...

1 Develop a storyboard from what you can remember of the tale on pages 185–6. Use a pencil to sketch out the frames. Try to use at least eight frames in your storyboard. The more detail you give, the easier the following extended writing task will be. **WS**

## EXTENSION TASK...

2 Use your storyboard to write the story from the point of view of one of the accused. Write in a way that would convince a judge listening to the plea. **WS**

## The king's interest

Eventually, the king began to take an interest in the law, as Source G shows. From 1200 onwards, the idea of trial by ordeal was being replaced by the jury system that is familiar today. The idea of a fair trial was also made part of the Magna Carta, signed by King John in 1215.

SOURCE G

Money was one of the main reasons why justice was administered at all. The king was entitled to keep the fines paid for minor offences and to confiscate the possessions of anyone convicted of a capital offence.

**An extract from a modern history book.**

# TASKS...

1 What reasons do you think there were for the king passing a law in the Middle Ages? Write down as many reasons as you can why we pass laws today. Then compare them to your answers for the Middle Ages.

## Plenary

Why do you think that laws change over time?

Make a brief list of all the technology we have today that makes proving a person's guilt easier than in medieval times.

If we did not have modern technology, what changes would we need to make to our laws? Does this explain the ways in which people were proved guilty of a crime in the Middle Ages?

# WHY DID MEDIEVAL PEOPLE TRAVEL?

**Objectives**

By the end of this section you will be able to answer these questions.
• Why did medieval people travel around England?
• What were the problems of travelling in the Middle Ages?
• Why did travel become increasingly popular?

## Starter

*How many times have you heard someone in your family say: 'The car's broken down again'? In the Middle Ages this wasn't a problem. Engines hadn't been invented!*

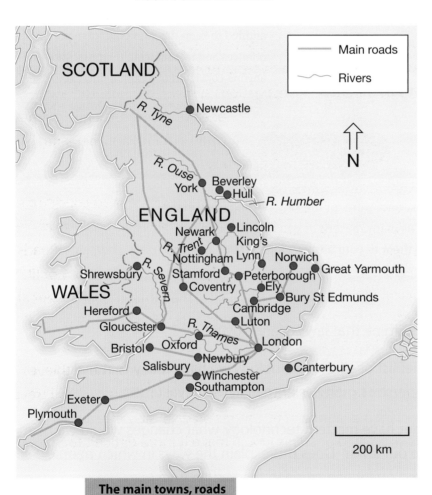

**The main towns, roads and rivers of medieval Britain, c.1400.**

*What changes do you think would happen to your town if there was no motorised transport at all? Write down how not having any motorised transport for a week would affect you. Now write down how not having any motorised transport for a year would affect you. How are your two lists different?*

## Travel in the Middle Ages

For most people in the Middle Ages, it was unusual to travel more than ten miles. However, travelling short distances was very common. Most ordinary people knew exactly where their local market was and how quickly they could get to it on foot. Sometimes, traders would bring special and unusual goods to the local markets. So for most people, there was no need to risk the dangers of travelling long distances by road.

Medieval roads were not like the ones we have today. There were fewer of them and the condition of most of them was very poor. Ever since the Romans left Britain in AD 410, the methods of building reliable roads had been almost forgotten. Many roads were little more than well-worn dirt tracks. Rain and snow turned these tracks into mud, making them impossible to pass. In 1499, a glove merchant from Aylesbury drowned in a two-metre hole in the road that he had mistaken to be a puddle. Investigations showed the hole to have been dug by a local miller, who could not find another source of clay.

Even if someone was willing to risk the journey, there was a problem of knowing exactly where you were. Few people could read or write, so there was little point in having signposts to guide a traveller's way. Any one wanting to travel was either familiar with the route or asked locals as they passed through villages. Travellers even had their own saint to protect them, St Christopher.

**The problems of a traveller in the medieval period.**

Apart from the road conditions, there were other dangers of travelling long distances. Roads connecting towns were not lit. Also, the transportation went at very low speeds, making travellers easy targets for highway thieves. These thieves were so dangerous that in 1285 the king ordered all bushes and trees be removed for a distance of 60 metres on each side of a road that connected market towns. This would make it more difficult for a thief to hide close to the road.

160 persons and more, all dressed in the form of war with light helmets, long swords and other weapons, hid under a large hedge next to the highway and lay in wait for William Tresham from midnight to the hour of six, at which time William appeared. They attacked him and smote him through the body and foot and more. He died. And they gave him many more deadly wounds and cut his throat.

**This extract, taken from the records of Parliament, details the problems of a traveller from Northampton to London in 1450.**

Not everyone travelled by road. Goods brought in to the country by ship were unloaded at crowded ports in the east of England. Onward journeys were made by boat along the major rivers of the country whenever the goods needed were too numerous, too bulky or just too heavy to go by road. However, when the river became too shallow or a different route was needed, then all the goods had to be unloaded and road transport used, no matter how unreliable.

SOURCE C

Most people who did travel were either those who were privileged or who made a living from travelling on the roads of England. Traders were the most frequent travellers. Carrying different goods on packhorses between towns, they provided all the goods that the people of a local area could not provide for themselves.

**A thirteenth-century painting of packhorses carrying wool.**

SOURCE D

Travellers often lose their way and go ways which are unknown. Therefore knots are made in the branches of trees and bushes to mark the highway.

**A traveller's description of the road markings c.1400.**

In 1484 William Naynow, an Exeter carrier, said he had been travelling between London and Exeter for over 35 years. He carried letters, pewter vessels and money – in fact, anything that people wanted to send.

These goods were sold in the weekly markets or at the fairs held once or twice a year. So many traders and travellers attended these fairs that they became special events. High-class traders dressed in their finery and riding expensive horses, selling the finest silks, cloth and rare spices, met in the same places as pedlars, jugglers and street musicians to swap news and tell stories over a jug of ale at the many inns in the town.

A contemporary illustration of a rich merchant.

Inns were not places to stay in for long. They were often dirty and flea-ridden. They attracted those who had an eye for a bargain and an ear for gossip. However, for the wary traveller the inn was a place to find company for the dangerous onward journey.

Travellers arriving at an inn, and the bedrooms they would have to share at night.

Even royalty found travelling difficult. In the Middle Ages, kings knew the value of being seen by the people they ruled, and so journeys around the country were not unusual. However, they were planned with great precision. Servants would go to the destination weeks before the king to announce the king's arrival and make sure all was well. This was an expensive pleasure for the host, as the king would bring many servants and bodyguards with him, and they all had to be fed and accommodated.

A medieval painting showing a travelling carriage for women in the royal family.

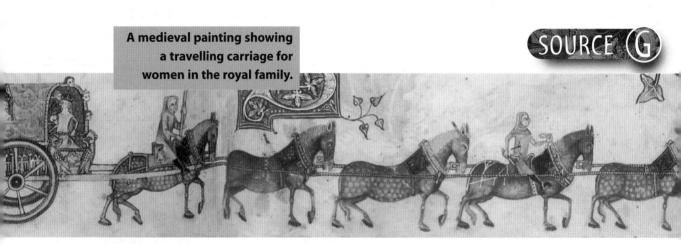

Those travelling on the journey were well guarded by the nobles riding horseback around the carriage. But the carriages themselves were very uncomfortable, because they did not have any springs to stop their passengers from feeling all the bumps and holes in the roads. The most a group would travel in a day was about 40 kilometres (see Source G as an example). But this was still safer and quicker than walking, as Source H shows. (By comparison, a lone horseman might travel about 56 kilometres a day.)

Travelling by foot took a long time, and was by no means safe.

## SOURCE 1

**An image from the Middle Ages of people on a pilgrimage.**

Other people travelled for religious reasons (as Chapter 4, pages 113–119 explains). In the Middle Ages, the Church encouraged travellers to seek out holy relics in places such as Canterbury, as Source I shows. Monasteries were expected to open their doors to tired travellers. Here the travellers would receive a basic meal and bed. It was not much, but it was shelter from the dangers of the open road.

## TASKS...

1  Using the information from pages 188–193, create a medieval snakes and ladders travel game.

   **a)** Draw out a 30 cm by 30 cm box. Divide it into 100 squares by drawing lines across and down every 3 cm. Number all the squares in a sequence, remembering that to play the game all the numbers must follow each other – that is, don't start a new line on the left of the game when you get to 11; the numbers will need to go from right to left (see the grid below). **WS**

| 21 | 22 | 23 | 24 | 25 | 26 | 27 | 28 | 29 | 30 |
|----|----|----|----|----|----|----|----|----|----|
| 20 | 19 | 18 | 17 | 16 | 15 | 14 | 13 | 12 | 11 |
| 1  | 2  | 3  | 4  | 5  | 6  | 7  | 8  | 9  | 10 |

   **b)** In square 1, write the name of your town. In square 100, write the name of a town some distance away from where you live. This is where your travellers will be going.

   **c)** On your game board you need to have five snakes (five problems) and five ladders (five good things). Look at the information on pages 188–193, and write down on a piece of paper your 'snakes' and your 'ladders'. Not all the problems will be as bad as each other.

   **d)** Decide which is the worst problem and make that the longest 'snake'. The problem that would cause your travellers the least problem will be your shortest 'snake'. Do the same with your 'ladders'. The event that will help your travellers most will be the longest ladder.

   **e)** When you have put on your snakes and ladders, have a go at playing your game!

**2** Using the snakes and ladders game that you have created, write a diary of your travellers' experiences as they pass through the towns and countryside of medieval England. Make sure you show the reasons why people wanted to travel, despite the problems. **WS**

## Plenary

The population of England during the Middle Ages was very low, fewer than 5 million people. Today our population is over 58 million. Draw a Venn diagram like the one below, showing all the advantages and disadvantages of travelling in *modern* Britain. In the overlap put any factors that are both good and bad.

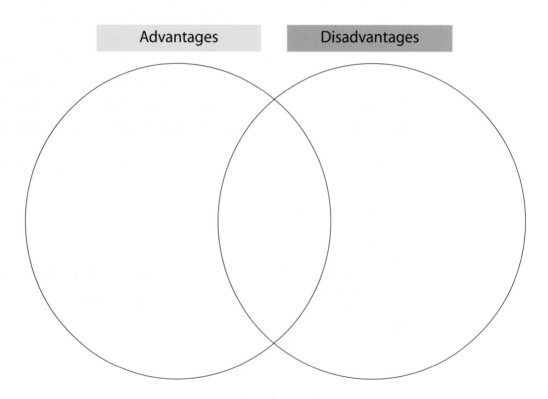

Advantages        Disadvantages

How would this diagram be different for the Middle Ages? Draw another Venn diagram and now put in all the advantages and disadvantages of travelling in medieval Britain.

# WHAT COMPARISONS CAN WE MAKE ABOUT LIFE IN THE MIDDLE AGES AND LIFE TODAY?

**Objectives**

By the end of this section you will be able to answer these questions.
- How was everyday life in the Middle Ages different to everyday life now?
- Why was daily life such a struggle for people in the Middle Ages?
- Why was it difficult for people in the Middle Ages to change the way they lived?

## Starter

*Throughout this chapter, we have looked at how hard life was for some of the people who lived in the Middle Ages. Things were very different then, and even the simplest things could take a long time.*

*How hard do you think your life is? Think about a normal week during term time. Work out carefully how many hours in a working week you spend in a classroom with a teacher (don't count the breaks!). Once you have done that, list how much free time you have to do what you want.*

*What do you need to consider to decide whether your life is hard or not?*

## Interpretations

- Would you agree or disagree with the statement?

- What do you need to prove the statement right or wrong? How would you go about proving it?

'Everyday life in the Middle Ages was hard.'

All historians need to interpret what they know, so what have you learned from this chapter that will help you to answer the key question: 'What was life like in the Middle Ages?'

SOURCE A

I work hard. I go out at daybreak driving the oxen to the field, and I yoke them to the plough. Even in deepest winter I dare not linger at home, for fear of my lord. But every day I must plough a full acre or more. I have a boy driving the oxen with a goad iron, who is hoarse with cold and shouting. And I do more also. I have to fill the oxen's bins with hay and water for them, and take out the litter. Mighty hard work it is, for I am not free.

**The working day of a medieval peasant.**

SOURCE B

**Rural workers. They worked outside on the land, as well as doing jobs like spinning wool.**

SOURCE C

SOURCE D

**Plague victims being buried, 1349.**

The king needed more money to pay for the war in France. In 1377, he introduced a poll tax. Everybody over the age of fifteen had to pay.

**From a modern textbook.**

💡 Look at Sources A to D. What do you think these sources tell you about everyday life for people living in the countryside in the Middle Ages?

If we are going to answer the question at the beginning of this chapter, '*What was life like in the Middle Ages?*', we need to understand how people lived in both the countryside and the towns.

There were more people who had to work for their living than there were people who were rich, and more who lived in the countryside than lived in towns.

💡 Look at Sources E and F, then compare them to Sources A to D. What similarities and differences do you see?

I have been round all the drapers' shops in Norwich and I can't buy any cloth good enough for a dress. Everything is too simple in colour and quality. Would you please get me three yards and a quarter of something you think would suit me? Choose whichever colour you like.

**A letter from the wife of a rich landowner to her husband, 1465.**

There was no dressing up, nor music, nor singing. There were no loud sports. Only board games, chess and card games were allowed.

**A description, written in about 1450, of how the death of the master of the house affected the Christmas celebrations.**

💡 What do you need to think about when you are using sources like these?

When thinking about sources, you need to consider the following.

● *Nature* – what type of source it is (for example, a letter, a painting, a poem and so on).
● *Origin* – who produced the source and when.
● *Purpose* – why this source was produced and for whom.

In the Middle Ages, few people could read and write. Only the really rich and those who had decided to become monks or nuns were literate. Ordinary people leave few traces of their lives, because much of their communication was spoken. There was nothing that we would use today to record sound, so what we know of everyday life we have to get from sources that show people going about their normal lives.

# TASKS...

**1 a)** Read the following poem. It is called 'Piers Plowman' and comes from the fourteenth century.

*I have no penny to buy **pullets**,
nor geese nor pigs, but [I have] two green cheeses,
a few **curds** of cream, a cake of oatmeal,
two loaves of beans and bran, baked for my children;
but I have parsley and pot herbs and plenty of cabbages,
a cow and a calf.*

*This is the little we must live on till the **Lammas** season.
Poor folks in **hovels**,
charged with children and overcharged by landlords,
what they may save by spinning they spend on rent,
on milk, or on a meal to make porridge.*

### Key words

**Pullets** Young chickens.

**Curds** Solids from milk.

**Lammas** The period of time from 1 August to 29 September.

**Hovel** A small miserable house.

**b)** With a partner, think about the 'message' the poem tries to put across. In your exercise book, write down any questions about the poem that come to mind.

**2** Draw a mind map like the one below. Use the rest of the information you have read in this chapter to say whether you think things did or did not change over this period. Make sure you put down at least one reason for your decision. **WS**

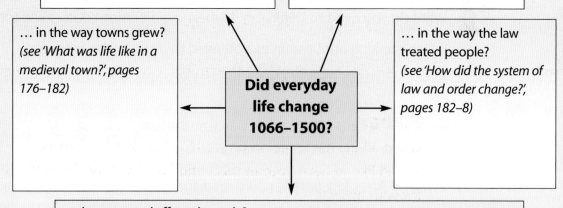

… in the way that people lived?
*(see 'What was it like to live in the Middle Ages?', pages 162–171)*

… in the way that people were treated?
*(see 'What was life like in the countryside?', pages 172–6)*

… in the way towns grew?
*(see 'What was life like in a medieval town?', pages 176–182)*

**Did everyday life change 1066–1500?**

… in the way the law treated people?
*(see 'How did the system of law and order change?', pages 182–8)*

… the way travel affected people?
*(see 'Why did medieval people travel?', pages 188–194)*

# TASKS...

**3** You have been invited to spend a week in the Middle Ages, but you need time to consider this invitation. Draw a Venn diagram like the one below to show:

- your reasons for wanting to live in the Middle Ages in one circle
- your reasons for not wanting to live in the Middle Ages in the other circle
- aspects you are not sure about in the overlap area. **WS**

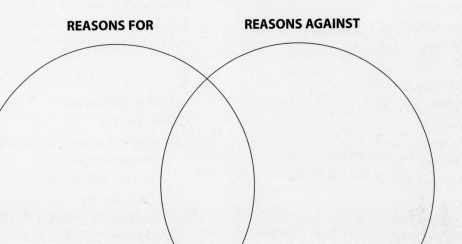

**REASONS FOR**        **REASONS AGAINST**

## EXTENSION TASK...

**4** Using what you have learned throughout this chapter, explain in writing whether you agree or disagree with the statement that *'Everyday life in the Middle Ages was hard.'* You may like to look back to Chapter 2 (page 73), which will give you some help with this writing. **WS**

## Plenary

Given all the evidence on pages 161–197, do you think you would like to have lived in this period of time? List the reasons for your answer.

# Index